Lives in Cricket: No 17

Fuller Pilch
A Straightforward Man

Brian Rendell

First published in Great Britain by
Association of Cricket Statisticians and Historians
Cardiff CF11 9XR
© ACS, 2010

Brian Rendell has asserted his right under the Copyright, Designs and Patents Act 1988 to be identified as the author of this work.

All Rights Reserved. No part of this publication may be reproduced, stored in a retrieval system, or transmitted in any form, or by any means, electronic, mechanical, photocopying, recording or otherwise without the prior permission in writing of the Copyright holders, nor be otherwise circulated in any form, or binding or cover other than in which it is published and without a similar condition including this condition being imposed on the subsequent publisher.

British Library Cataloguing-in-Publication Data.
A catalogue record for this book is available from the British Library.

ISBN: 978 1 905138 97 5
Typeset by Limlow Books

Contents

Preface   5

Chapter One	The Brothers Pilch	9
Chapter Two	Bowling revolution	11
Chapter Three	Batting evolution	14
Chapter Four	Found by a 'Suffolk spirit'	18
Chapter Five	Round-Arm bowling proves its case	21
Chapter Six	Bury St Edmunds defeat MCC	26
Chapter Seven	Committed to East Anglia, for now	29
Chapter Eight	A year of indecision	34
Chapter Nine	Champion of England, Part One	36
Chapter Ten	Champion of England, Part Two	39
Chapter Eleven	Norfolk: the final years	43
Chapter Twelve	Town Malling and Mr Pickwick	49
Chapter Thirteen	Kent become the greatest team in England	55
Chapter Fourteen	A new Champion of England	60
Chapter Fifteen	Attracted by the seaside charms of Sussex	62
Chapter Sixteen	The growing influence of the Beverley Club	67
Chapter Seventeen	The birth of Canterbury Cricket Week	74
Chapter Eighteen	William Martingell joins Fuller at Canterbury	81
Chapter Nineteen	William Pilch joins Uncle Fuller at Canterbury	85
Chapter Twenty	William Clarke creates the All-England Eleven	91
Chapter Twenty-One	The new St Lawrence Ground	96
Chapter Twenty-Two	Three cheers for the 'stale' men	102
Chapter Twenty-Three	Fuller's final seasons	106
Chapter Twenty-Four	Umpire, coach, groundsman, bat-maker and mine host	117
Chapter Twenty-Five	A pipe in Fuller Pilch's back parlour	121
Chapter Twenty-Six	A pension and a monument	127

Acknowledgements		134
Bibliography		135
Appendix:	Career Statistics	139
Index		142

Preface

My interest in the cricket career of Fuller Pilch began when I was researching material for a history of nineteenth-century single-wicket contests played for the 'Championship of England' and how they appealed to the public in comparison to the famous bare-knuckle prize-fights of the time. I knew that no biography had ever been written of this great cricketer, not even as part of the ACS 'Famous Cricketers' series. He had, though, won the title 'Champion of England' in 1833 and remained unchallenged for five years, admired and respected by the hundreds of spectators who came to see him play. Thus he consolidated his position as the premier batsman in club and representative cricket at Lord's and elsewhere. According to William Denison, writing in 1846 in *Sketches of the Players*: 'There has been no man, having played as many matches, who has approached him in effectiveness and safety of style, or in the number of runs he obtained.'

The idea of a long overdue biography grew as my investigations seemed to show that, despite being recognised by modern historians as an important figure, he was usually overshadowed by that colossus of Victorian cricket, the great all-rounder Alfred Mynn, in much the same way as the technically correct scoring-machine Geoffrey Boycott was overshadowed by the exploits of Ian Botham almost 150 years later.

When I began my research for the material for a biography, I soon learned why nobody had tried to write one before. Fuller Pilch was a very private man. He had never married and there was no paper trail to follow. He left no diary, no letters remained in the possession of descendants waiting to be discovered and their contents revealed. In his book *Seventy-One Not Out*, William Caffyn described him as 'a remarkably quiet man, with no conversation, and never seemed happier than when behind a churchwarden pipe, all by himself.' His obituary in the *Kentish Gazette* stated that he 'was a man of somewhat reserved manners'. At the height of his fame, the *Norwich Mercury* wrote that 'his manly, straight-forward, yet unassuming conduct, his energy, his cool determined courage, and last but not least, his unimpeachable truth and honesty, have gained for him the respect and confidence of his employers as well as of his associates.' The *Kent Herald* agreed that 'he was relied upon by the patrons of cricket as not only a man who would do his best in the game but would do it with a simple unassuming modesty, which contrasted most favourably with other and lesser stars in the cricket world.'

It seemed unlikely that I would find enough material to write an interesting history of such a paragon of virtues. Then I came across a brief glimpse of an unexpected aspect of his personality which suggested my efforts might not be in vain. He played cricket in an age when wagers were won and lost at matches almost everywhere and, in a rare moment when his guard was down, he boasted to author and friend Frederick Gale that he was often involved. In *The Game of Cricket*, Gale reported him as saying, 'They used to offer to take a sovereign from me before going in, and pay me a shilling a run; and a good thing I made of it sometimes.' He then added, 'some of them, they would give me the shilling a run and my own sovereign back too very often, if Kent won.' Not exactly the Hansie Cronje of the nineteenth century perhaps, just sound business transactions conducted by a man confident in his own ability. Such risk-taking suggests that there was more to him than might at first appear, and explains why at the end of his life he was in penury, lodging with his nephew and family, and dependent upon a pension of one pound a week from the Beverley Club in Canterbury.

Even then, putting something together into the format for the Association's 'Lives in Cricket' series was going to be much more difficult than I had at first imagined. There seemed no better place to start than by analysing all the matches in which Fuller Pilch appeared as recorded in the Association's seven volumes of 'Important Cricket Matches' covering the years 1820 to 1863. For details of other matches I turned to the first five volumes of Frederick Lillywhite's *Scores and Biographies*, although even these would not include every match in which Fuller had appeared, as not all club records had been preserved. Then I covered the bare bones of matches with extracts from press reports where they were available. With the help of historians and librarians from Norfolk, Suffolk, Yorkshire, Oxford, Cambridge, Nottingham and Kent, a picture of a career began to emerge. In presenting that career I have kept to the chronological order of the matches in which Fuller Pilch played, ignoring any difference in their status, so that the extraordinary diversity of his engagements, switching from team to team and place to place, can be fully appreciated.

Fuller Pilch was at, or near, the peak of his profession for perhaps twenty years. He played in almost every important match of his time, typically appearing at about fourth in the batting order. His contribution to the growth of the popularity of cricket was immense. He was a practising tailor from a family of tailors but he made most of his living playing cricket and it cannot be denied that he always went where the money was. This usually meant joining clubs with wealthy sponsors where he would be paid for appearing in matches, coaching club members, acting as publican of a nearby inn, and even taking on the duties of groundsman. His early reputation was earned in Norfolk, Suffolk, Cambridge and by regular appearances at Lord's. Then he was lured to Kent with the prospect of even bigger earnings and played an important role in the creation of the greatest cricket event outside the big matches at Lord's in the middle of the nineteenth century, the Canterbury Cricket Week. In many ways his career can perhaps be compared to that of a twentieth-century player who sold his reputation and services to Packer's 'World Series' or the 'rebel' tours to South Africa, or his twenty-first-century equivalent who sells them to the highest bidder for his employment in money-making Twenty20 tournaments. Fortunately for Fuller he was seeking employment as a professional cricketer in the first half of the nineteenth-century and not in the twenty-first. If his home club had no fixture that required his services he always reserved the right to augment his earnings by accepting any engagement to play anywhere for any team that came calling. In 2010 such a mercenary attitude attracted the criticism of ex-England captain Mike Atherton, writing in *The Times*, who called it 'Modern cricket *in extremis*' and censured any cricketer for selling his talent in this way as a player 'with no feelings for the club, the supporters or players, attempting to do a professional job for which he was paid handsomely.' Unlike the modern international cricketer, Fuller's window of opportunity to cash in on his reputation was restricted to less than five months of the English summer.

England was at war with Napoleon when Fuller Pilch was born and the future King George IV was still Prince Regent when he first played cricket as a boy. The Crimean War was at its height when he retired and Queen Victoria had been on the throne for thirty-two years when he died in 1870. In his early career players arrived at matches between towns and villages by coach, wagon, dray, on horseback or on foot. For longer journeys a stagecoach was hired, with half the team on the roof. Such coaches were known as a 'Godpermit', short for 'God permit I arrive safely' because of the dangers of travel by road. The number of stagecoach journeys Fuller would have to make every season was remarkable, some of them taking 24 hours or even longer, in conditions as far removed from the team buses and business-class air travel enjoyed by the modern international cricketer as it is possible to imagine. By the time he retired, a network of railways had been constructed that covered England so that teams could be carried between cities and towns hundreds of miles apart in a matter of hours rather than days.

As a young batsman Pilch had to learn to deal with the problems posed by skilful under-arm bowling before adjusting his technique to master the new dangers presented by the revolutionary round-arm method. Round-arm bowling was illegal according to MCC until 1828 when a limited version was written into the Laws, but it was condoned for many years before that by clubs with bowlers practising a version they believed satisfied the confusing Law that was supposed to be in operation. It was finally given the green light in 1835. By then batsmen had started to experiment with pads to protect their legs, worn originally out of sight under their trousers, and padded gloves to prevent damage to fingers. Heads were already being protected by top hats, usually black, sometimes white.

After retirement from cricket, Fuller Pilch could be found most days in his parlour at the Saracen's Head Inn in Canterbury, where from 1855 to 1866 he was joint landlord with his nephew. It was there that Frederick Gale sought him out and persuaded the veteran to reminisce about his glory years on the playing fields of Kent and beyond. Gale published the results of their conversations in *The Game of Cricket* in 1887. And there, at last, we can hear an echo of the voice of Fuller Pilch.

Bromley, Kent
October, 2010

This village sign, erected in Oxwick Road, Horningtoft, recorded Fuller Pilch on its right hand panel.

Chapter One
The Brothers Pilch

Fuller Pilch was born in a cottage close to the village church, St Edmund's, at Horningtoft, midway between Norwich and King's Lynn in Norfolk's fertile boulder-clay country, on 17 March 1804.[1] He was the sixth of ten children born to Nathaniel Pilch and Frances Fuller who were married on Christmas Eve 1792. Both surnames were derived from the Norfolk cloth-making industries.[2] Fuller had three older brothers, Nathaniel, William and John Fuller, who died in 1797 before reaching his first birthday. He also had two older sisters, Susanna and Frances. There were four children after Fuller, two of whom died very young.

There are no records to confirm that Nathaniel Pilch senior, who kept a tailor's shop in Holt, ever played cricket, but there may have been cricketers in his wife's family as Volume One of *Scores and Biographies* includes, for the 1797 season, a 'Grand Cricket Match' played at Swaffham racecourse for a purse of 500 guineas 'between Eleven Men of all England against Thirty-three of the County of Norfolk' and the Norfolk team included John Fuller, James Fuller, Bayfield Fuller and Ben Fuller.

The three Pilch brothers, Nathaniel, William and Fuller, all grew up to become good cricketers, all right-handed batsmen, with the youngest maturing into the greatest player of his generation. Nathaniel and William played regularly for Holt and later for other villages in north Norfolk including Brinton, Brisley, Litcham, Blickling and Hingham, up to 1848. Both were in the Norfolk team in 1820 with Fuller when he made his debut at Lord's, aged only sixteen, and all three brothers played together for Holt in 1821 and 1822. But it would then be another seven years before they were re-united on the field in a Norfolk versus Suffolk match at Norwich in 1829; this time they were on opposite sides as Fuller had qualified to play for Suffolk after being engaged as the professional at Bury St Edmunds.

Over the next twenty years the brothers still occasionally appeared in representative matches either against or alongside each other. Despite moving to Kent in 1835, Fuller never lost contact with his roots and even at the height of his fame enjoyed returning to Norfolk and Suffolk from time

---

1   He was 'baptized privately' the following day, according to the parish records, so he may have been a sickly infant.
2   A 'fuller' is or was a person involved in the scouring or thickening of cloth. A 'pilcher' was a maker or seller of pilches, odd-sounding outer garments 'made of skin dressed with hair'. In the nineteenth century, the surname Pilch was almost entirely concentrated in East Norfolk: Fuller was common in eastern England but rare in the west.

The Brothers Pilch

This fading page in the Horningtoft parish records notes Fuller Pilch's birth on 17 March 1804 and his baptism the following day.

to time to play village and club cricket. In 1845 the family tradition was continued when Nathaniel's son William joined his uncle Fuller in Kent where he also developed into a fine all-round cricketer in his adopted county.

Nathaniel and William were naturally very proud of their younger brother Fuller's outstanding achievements on the cricket field, but after he moved to Kent they could only learn the details second-hand through the columns of newspapers. It may have been that fraternal pride that prompted the brothers to conceive of the idea of recording batsmen's scores as reported in *Bell's Life* during the summer and compiling a list of averages at the end of the season, knowing that Fuller's figures would feature at, or near, the top. They were published in *Bell's Life* for the first time in 1840 and again in 1841, but the idea had proved so popular that from 1842 other readers began to submit their own tables, and disagreement ensued regarding accuracy. The arguments became even more heated after 1843 when bowlers' figures were included, and in 1846 the publishers of *Bell's Life* appointed their own members of staff to produce 'official' tables.

Cricket statisticians owe an enormous debt of gratitude to Nathaniel and William Pilch for being the first lovers of cricket to draw attention to the value of statistics when comparing the performance of players.

Church Road, Horningtoft in 2010. The house on the left occupies the site of the cottages where Fuller Pilch was born in 1804. The church where he was baptised by Rev George Norris is just visible through the trees.

Chapter Two
Bowling revolution

In order to understand and appreciate the batting achievements of Fuller Pilch we must first have a clear idea of the bowling methods that he faced. These were very different to those employed in the modern game. Bowling methods evolved and changed very quickly during the first 15 years of his career, including variations of under-arm and round-arm bowling, and he had to adapt and adjust his own batting style to deal with them as the seasons progressed.

When cricket was first being played in the fields and on the village greens of England, bowlers propelled the ball towards wickets by rolling it under-arm as fast as possible along the ground. The batsman, using a stick that was curved at the bottom end similar to a modern hockey stick, would attempt to strike the ball past a defending ring of fieldsmen. Due to the nature of the uneven ground between the wickets, the ball would occasionally bounce up over the batsman's stick and knock his stumps over. Bowlers eventually realised that they could achieve this effect deliberately by slowing down their delivery and tossing the ball forward in a manner which became known as 'lobbing'. Batsmen, frustrated by the ease in which the bouncing ball could elude the frame of their curved sticks, had them made straighter and wider. Bowlers responded by moving their arm away from their bodies to give room for the hand to twist and spin the ball to make it change direction after landing in front of the batsman. The hand was still well below the elbow and there could be no argument that the method was anything other than under-arm. Regulations concerning the size of a bat were introduced in 1771, according to Peter Wynne-Thomas in his book *A History of Cricket: From the Weald to the World,* 'as a result of switching the bowling from along the ground to first bounce to the batsman sometime in the 1760s.' Keith Warsop has recently presented in *The Cricket Statistician* evidence that 'pitching the ball rather than rolling it along the ground can be dated back possibly to before the 1720s.'

In the early 1780s David Harris developed the art of persistent length bowling. A list of batting averages from 1771 to 1864, compiled by Keith Warsop for his article 'Batting evolution – its effect on run-scoring' in *The Cricket Quarterly* in 1966 tells us a great deal about the initial success of Harris and other late eighteenth-century bowlers at curtailing batsmen's freedom to score. Warsop clarified the compilation of his tables by explaining that he wanted to show how the players compared against others of their generation. He had, therefore, included figures from all matches which would be considered first-class today, and many that would not but where the quality of the players rather than the names of the teams had been the guide. The figures show that there was a decline in batting averages from 1780 to 1798, but after 1799, as batsmen improved their technique, the figures showed a steady increase. From 1799 to 1815 there were 17 averages over 30, from 1816 until 1826 there were 25 averages over 30, including three over 50 and eleven over 40. It is clear that bowlers in the early years of the nineteenth century were finding it increasingly difficult to keep batsmen from scoring.

A new bowling method was needed. Some adventurous bowlers realised that by extending the arm further away from their bodies, but still with the hand below the elbow, and then swinging the arm forward, they could significantly increase the speed of their deliveries. The next step was to raise the arm into a horizontal position, draw it further back and use a wide-sweeping motion to hurl it towards the wicket, thereby achieving real pace. To many this looked suspiciously like 'throwing' and the practice was frowned upon as it caused bad feelings between teams who had bowlers using the new method, called 'straight-arm', and those that did not. It was banned at Lord's but refused to go away and in 1816 MCC introduced a new Law intended to eliminate it from the game entirely: 'The ball must be delivered underhand, not thrown or jerked, with the hand below the elbow at the time of delivering the ball. If the arm is extended straight from the body, or the back part of the hand be uppermost when the ball is delivered, or the arm extended horizontally, the umpire shall call no ball.'

Many umpires were puzzled by the wording of the new Law and disagreed on how it was to be applied. Practitioners of straight-arm bowling, or 'round-arm' as it soon became known, refused to admit defeat and abandon their methods despite MCC disapproval. In fact, the method gained in popularity and began to spread slowly around the counties, in particular at Brighton where Sussex, with William Lillywhite bowling slow-medium round-arm and James Broadbridge using the faster version, developed into the leading team of the 1820s.

Reformers at Lord's forced the diehards to reconsider their opposition and in 1827 three experimental matches were arranged between Sussex, who were allowed to bowl round-arm, and a team under the title 'All England' selected by MCC from the best players available, including the up-and-coming Fuller Pilch as an all-rounder. All the players were expected to abide by the latest numbered version of the Laws but only the 'All England' bowlers were to be bound by Law 10 which had been rewritten but was even more confusing than before: 'The ball must be bowled (not thrown or jerked) and delivered underhand with the hand below the elbow. But if the ball be jerked or the arm extended from the body horizontally, and any part of the back of the hand be uppermost, or the hand horizontally extended when the ball shall be delivered, the umpire shall call "No Ball".'

The matches were played at Sheffield, Lord's and Brighton and enjoyed by large crowds. Round-arm bowling was here to stay and finally MCC backed down and simplified the Law in time for the start of the 1828 season, so that it now read: 'The ball shall be bowled. If it be thrown or jerked, or if any part of the hand or arm be above *the elbow* [my italics] at the time of delivery, the umpire shall call "No Ball".'

Batsmen were now expected to cope with this limited form of round-arm bowling on a regular basis and run-getting was reduced dramatically. Only Fuller Pilch could compare with the older generation of batsmen. Warsop's figures show that in the seven years from 1828 to 1834 there were only eleven annual batting averages over 20, with Fuller Pilch claiming more than half of them. And in the nine years from 1835 to 1843, after all restrictions to round-arm bowling were lifted when the word 'elbow' was changed by MCC to 'shoulder' in Law 10, there were only 15 averages over 20, seven of them from Fuller Pilch, while only Felix featured twice. Those averages may seem low to the modern reader but it should be remembered that, throughout Fuller Pilch's career, team innings totals rarely exceeded 200, frequently never reached three figures, and that runs came slowly at between 150-200 per day, mainly in singles, with twos, threes and, before boundary lines existed, all-run fours, fives or more, celebrated by the spectators as excitedly as sixes are cheered in today's T20 run-fests.

Chapter Three
Batting evolution

In the days when only under-arm bowling was lawful, batsmen had usually remained standing up straight at their crease, legs apart and bat raised, while waiting for the ball to come towards them, giving them time to select an appropriate stroke. One of the most admired strokes was called the 'draw', when, if the batsman was sure that the ball was shooting flat and straight along the ground he would watch it go past his front leg and then glance the ball between his legs to the on-side. Some bolder batsmen would even lift the front leg as high as possible to make it easier to swing the bat and strike the ball past square leg. Not as spectacular as a 'Dilshan Dilscoop' perhaps, or even Kevin Pietersen's 'flamingo', but it shows that Georgian batsmen were as inventive as their twenty-first century T20 counterparts.

The speed and bounce of good-length round-arm deliveries eliminated the 'draw' and many other previously successful strokes from the batsman's repertoire as it invariably trapped the batsman flat-footed in front of the stumps with little or no time to prepare any sort of effective response. Fuller Pilch had the answer. Just over six feet tall, with long legs and arms, he would stretch as far forward as possible from an upright stance to meet the ball with his bat just after it landed and before it could bounce higher or shoot. This became famous as 'Pilch's poke' but Frederick Gale insisted that it was much more than that because the stroke could bring runs while Fuller was 'smothering the ball before it has time to rise and break, and placing it to the 'off' or the 'on', with the greatest apparent ease.' Fuller developed his forward play even further and was able to place less accurate bowling through the field on the offside with the earliest form of the classic cover-drive, described by Gale in *The Game of Cricket* thus: 'I hardly ever saw him let off an off-ball which was wide of the wicket, and he had a tremendous hit in front of point, between middle and cover, which gained him many a four or five runs.'

The finest exponent of round-arm bowling, often round the wicket, throughout much of Fuller's career was William Lillywhite and they were involved in many duels over the years. The *Bury and Norwich Post* reported:

> Pilch, with his long forward reach, would stretch forward and meet Lillywhite's balls at the pitch and wither lay them dead under his bat or drive them a little back according to the length and his power to command them. Lillywhite, with change of pace and elevation, would diminish or increase the length inch by inch until Pilch was in doubt whether to play forward or back, in the latter case having the least

possible time to guard. 'If I can catch Pilch in two minds what to do', said the artful dodger, 'I shall have him to a certainty.'

Wishful thinking or bravado on the part of the bowler, it seems, as it didn't quite work out like that. The pair faced each other in 89 first-class matches and out of 165 of Fuller's innings, Lillywhite is known to have dismissed him on only 49 occasions, although it is likely that Fuller was caught on other occasions off Lillywhite when the bowler was not credited with the wicket.

At Canterbury in 1845, Fuller gave Gale a lesson in batting, beginning with taking guard:

> There now, here's the wicket as you are a-going in to; you go behind the wicket and find out where the bowler's hand will be, get the middle stump in a line between yourself and the bowler's hand, and you sight the ground. Then ask for your block, and if you have hit it right, put your right foot firm behind the crease clear of the on-stump, and take your block right on the crease, and throw your left foot forward and keep your left shoulder up, and never let the bowler's hand be off it; and as long as you don't draw your left foot on the on-side you can't play with anything but a straight bat. Keep yourself free and firm; but be sure if you drop your shoulder or draw your left foot you are a dead man.

He then went on to give advice on making the off-drive:

> Don't be too anxious about hitting an off-ball until you are well set; and then, if you feel your hand and eye are together and know she is wide of the off-stump, throw your left leg forward and let her have it. I didn't do so myself, as I could reach her off or not, and make the drive, or place her where I could see an opening; it is safer, though less showy. You take care in playing forward against good bowling to watch the pace; for just as you are pleased as Punch at your defence, a good bowler will drop one shorter and slower, and it will be his turn to laugh if he bowls and catches you, as he very likely will.

Fuller had more to say about facing left-handed round-arm bowling:

> Take the guard to the bowler's hand as in right-hand bowling, and mind you don't play outside the ball when she breaks; try to watch the line of the pitch, and put the face of the bat on her, but you MUST learn that by PRACTICE; and all I can say is what the schoolmasters used to say to you over your Greek letters – and a very ugly family they are, I only saw them once – 'If you don't mind your book you will get the stick,' and if you don't learn to put the face of the bat on the ball off the left-hand bowler you will lose your wicket.

Even Richard Daft was impressed by the Pilch technique, although Pilch had retired before Daft began playing, so he never actually saw him out in the middle. In *Kings of Cricket* he commented: 'but I remember seeing him have some practice once at Canterbury when I played there, and being much struck with the gracefulness of his forward play.'

Fuller Pilch scored nearly 14,000 runs, perhaps more, in all grades of cricket in his career, including ten centuries, in an age when three figures was as rare as a triple-hundred is today, but there was one stroke that he never mastered. Nicholas Felix learnt of it by accident when researching for his 'scientific inquiry into the use of the Cricket Bat' titled *Felix on the Bat*. It appears in the section dealing with the correct stance that should be taken by a batsman when waiting to receive:

> I was invited to play in a match at Malling, near Maidstone, in the days when (under the auspicious patronage of Thomas Selby Esq, and other gentlemen of equal zeal) Fuller Pilch had the ground. The match [Town Malling v Kent 1836] being over in the early part of the third day, I accompanied him, with some of his patrons, to his little receiving-parlour in the High Street. The conversation happened to turn upon this Publication and then came a few pros and cons. Pilch was requested to assume his attitude of Play, with which (with his usual *suaviter in modo*)[3] he complied. He admitted the difficulty of preparing himself so immediately for the back cut as might be done by the bending of both knees. And it was a remark, that, with all his stupendous hitting, decision and reach, he could not make the back cut equal to the other parts of his batting; and it was agreed, that this circumstance arose from the fact of his keeping his right leg perfectly straight. Such an admission from such a Cricketer was not to be disregarded, and I trust I do not take advantage of this confession to the deterioration of his acknowledged skill; for, let our excellences be ever so bright, we are none of us perfect; no, not one.

One year later, thanks to an invention by Nicholas Felix, the skills of Fuller's batting technique were placed under scrutiny again, this time with a more positive result. Felix realised that net-practice bowlers lacked the accuracy and uniformity needed to help a batsman perfect a particular stroke. So he invented the *catapulta*, a mechanical contraption that could bowl balls on a length towards a batsman in the nets. One of several public demonstrations was arranged by William Caldecourt, the long-serving and popular practice bowler employed by MCC at Lord's, and a report duly appeared in the *The Sportsman* newspaper:

> The delightfully laid-out grounds at the Victoria Gardens, Gravesend, were numerously attended on Monday, October 9th, Caldecourt having announced his intention of bringing the newly-invented bowling-machine called the Catapulta into operation against the cricketers of Gravesend, on which occasion Fuller Pilch came from Town Malling to assist Caldecourt in the proceedings of the day. Nearly all the most famous batsmen of Gravesend and for many miles round

---

[3] From the Latin *suaviter in modo, fortiter in re*: gently in mode, firmly in action.

assembled at an early hour, and shortly after ten o'clock the machine was brought into play.

After a number of batsmen had tested themselves against the machine and had their stumps sent flying, frequently by the first ball they received, it was time for Fuller to step up and the report continued:

Much interest was excited on that celebrated batsman taking his stand against the bowling of the machine, which, by means of a screw, was made to imitate the fast bowling of Redgate. For some time all the balls were directed to the middle stump, but Pilch kept them away, demonstrating that the only method of preventing all straight balls from displacing the stumps was by playing either forward or back with an 'upright bat'. Caldecourt then tried various manoeuvres to get in a ball by varying the style of bowling; and although the striker might, perhaps, more than once have been caught out had he been playing in a match, yet, by the masterly manner in which he batted, he kept all the balls away from his wicket for a long time.

Fuller Pilch would be successful at keeping balls away from his wicket for the next seventeen years and his style of batting, admired and emulated whenever possible, became the benchmark for all new batsmen as they came forward into the game. He was the batting genius who truly bridged the gap between the old style cricket of Hambledon and the modern game of W.G.Grace.

Chapter Four
Found by a 'Suffolk spirit'

In a preview to the match to be played at Sheffield in 1828 featuring a combined Yorkshire, Leicestershire and Nottinghamshire eleven against an All-England team which included Fuller Pilch, the *Sheffield Mercury* claimed credit for Sheffield for the development of Pilch as a cricketer before he settled at Bury St Edmunds: 'This man was originally Norfolk bred; migrated to the north for bread and water at an early age, and learned to handle bats and balls at Sheffield where he became distinguished, and where he was found by a Suffolk spirit.'

In a crowded family home where his two elder brothers were already training under their father to follow him into the tailoring trade, it is not surprising that the younger boy, also training to be a tailor, but showing exceptional promise as a cricketer, was sent somewhere his cricket talents could be developed under more experienced guidance. Sheffield was a suitable place to go, where cricket was being played seriously and more regularly than in Norfolk, and there may have been relatives available to take him in. There appears to have been an ongoing relationship with the city for the Pilch family and Fuller's brother William would actually move there from Norfolk in later years. There is no record of Fuller playing at Sheffield before 1820, but eventually the sixteen-year-old returned to join his brothers at Lord's to play for Norfolk on July 24 that year.[4] This was the occasion when William Ward, who broke the record for highest individual score with 278 for MCC in the match, had been sufficiently impressed to declare: 'If that young Pilch goes on in his play, there is much promise in him.' Back in Norfolk, Fuller is recorded as playing at Holt with his brothers against Nottingham twelve months after the Lord's match, and then again twelve months after that, when they travelled to Nottingham for the return match on 29 July 1822. Thirteen months later he appeared again, but this time for Bury against Biggleswade at Cambridge. This was the first of 26 games that he played for the Suffolk town of Bury St Edmunds after he had settled there in 1823 and his reputation would eventually be celebrated in verse as part of a poem 'The Crack Eleven of England' that appeared in Pierce Egan's *Book of Sports*:

---

4   The MCC *v* Norfolk match is now regarded as first-class by the ACS. A search of the CricketArchive database shows that at the time only two younger players had appeared in first-class cricket. These were both fifteen-year-olds, John Beeston, who played for MCC *v* Middlesex at the old Lord's in 1794, and G.T.Smith, who played for Middlesex *v* Epsom at the new Lord's in 1815. Birth date records of this period are of course distinctly patchy.

> Another bold tailor, as fine a young man
> As e'er hit a ball and then afterwards ran,
> Is from Bury St. Edmunds, and Pilch they him call,
> In a few years 'tis thought he'll be better than all.
>
> At present his batting's a little too wild,
> Tho' the 'Nonpareil Hitter' he's sometimes been styled;
> So free and so fine, with the hand of a master,
> Spectators all grieve when he meets with disaster.

A report in the *Cambridge Independent Press* in 1823 of Fuller's first match for Bury at Cambridge, on 22 and 23 September, suggests that the move to Suffolk did not have a smooth start:

> Some delay took place in consequence of the Biggleswade club objecting to the bowling of a young man in the Bury club named Pilch, on the ground of not knowing who he was, and that he was not a regular member of the Bury club; although it appears they had accepted his name as one of the 11. His bowling is certainly very superior, and although the Biggleswade club really stood but little chance of success, it would doubtless have rendered the game of shorter duration. However, to arrange the matter, it was agreed that a case should be drawn up for the decision of the chairman of the Mary-le-bone club (W.Ward, Esq) as to whether they could object to Pilch's bowling; and another match was made, Pilch being debarred bowling. Some good batting as well as fielding was displayed on both sides, particularly the dexterous manner in which Pilch stumped out Mr D.Onslow, excited general admiration.

Being 'stumped out' does not mean that Fuller had added the skills of wicket-keeping to his repertoire, but that was how a batsman being run out by a fielder was recorded in the scorebooks of the time.

By the summer of 1824 Fuller was officially a member of the Bury club as its paid professional, and he appeared in both of the games against Biggleswade and two other matches with the Essex village of Pattiswick. In these early days of his career he was a very successful under-arm bowler and in the four matches he took 36 wickets. He also made his first known half-century, scoring 51 against Biggleswade.

Bury played two matches against Newmarket in 1825, winning both by an innings. In the second match Fuller made another half-century, a top score of 69 out of 188. The Bury club was earning a reputation as a team to be reckoned with and at the beginning of September an announcement appeared in the *Cambridge Independent Press*:

> The grand Match at Cricket between the Nottingham and Bury clubs, for 100 sovereigns a-side, will take place at Roughham Park, four miles from Bury, (on the Ipswich road) on Monday next. The Bury Club are allowed three given men, and have selected Brand, Esq., his servant

Matthews (a celebrated bowler) and another. We need scarcely add that extreme interest is excited. The stumps will be pitched at ten o'clock.

Nottingham had been beaten only once in their previous 19 matches and for that sort of wager their sponsors were confident enough to risk the effects on the team of two days coach travel. The home side played well and won by 33 runs thanks to a top score of 25 from Fuller in their second innings. The match was over in one day and attracted enormous enthusiasm in Suffolk, according to the *Bury and Norwich Post*: 'The game excited an unusual degree of interest with several 1000 persons attending; including the High Sheriff, the Duke of Grafton and their families and numerous assemblages of neighbouring gentry.'

The Bury club continued to grow in stature and at the start of the 1826 season announced in the *Bury and Norwich Post* that 'Practice would commence at 12 o'clock in the new cricket ground. Meeting at the Angel Inn when the company of Gentlemen desirous of becoming a member is particularly requested.' Gentlemen played cricket for fun but were always keen to improve their skills and would have expected that Fuller, as the club's professional, a tradesman by comparison, attended all the practice sessions. No doubt some of the gentlemen rewarded him for his instruction in addition to the basic fee he received from the club. As a young tailor starting out on his own, any extra income would have been gratefully received. Bury started their season playing two games in May at Cambridge against undergraduate sides. Their next recorded match was at Saffron Walden on 21 and 22 July, with the home team winning by 32 runs. On 14 August Bury were at home to Melford and Fuller came very close to recording the first century of his career with an unbeaten 91 out of 131. The big match that summer came four days later against 'Eleven Gentlemen from Newmarket, Cambridge and Saffron Walden' for a stake of £50. Bury won this easily, with Fuller making an unbeaten 82 out of their first innings of 150, and his skills were acknowledged in the *Bury and Norwich Post*: 'Pilch, as usual, sent the ball where he chose.'

Bury went to Saffron Walden again, on 28 and 29 August, and this time won by an innings. In the Saffron Walden side there was a great player from the Hambledon days of the eighteenth century, William Fennex, now 62, who had returned to settle in Suffolk. Fennex had played in the past for Sheffield clubs and he had been one of the earliest players to experiment with forward play. It is possible that he had coached the young Fuller when both were in Sheffield. The skills Fuller could have learned from Fennex enabled him to deal with the increasing amount of round-arm bowling that was finding its way into the game. In the return match at Newmarket against 'Eleven Gentlemen from Newmarket, Cambridge and Saffron Walden' on 8 and 9 September, Fuller top-scored with 48 out of 128 to help Bury win by an innings.

Many people had been impressed by the progress of the young Fuller Pilch and word reached Lord's where three experimental matches were being set up for the following year to test the legitimacy of round-arm bowling.

Chapter Five
Round-Arm bowling proves its case

The 1827 season would prove to be one of the most important years in the history of the cricket as well as an outstanding year for the Bury St Edmunds club. Fuller Pilch was at the heart of both.

He began with two games for Bury against the Cambridge undergraduates on May 17 and 18. In the first he made top score of 48 out of 86 in Bury's only innings, followed by one and nought in the second game in which a total of only 72 runs were scored by both sides. He was then called up for the first of the three 'trial' matches arranged by MCC to test out round-arm bowling in 'big match' conditions. Supporters of the round-arm method were determined to convince their opponents that it was not 'throwing' and offered no more danger of physical injury to batsmen than traditional under-arm.

Fuller travelled to Sheffield with another Bury player, the bowler William Mathews, to join the team chosen to represent All England and found the city in a state of great excitement at the prospect of the match due to start on Whit Monday. An advertisement had appeared on the front page of the *Sheffield Mercury*:

CRICKETING
THREE GRAND MATCHES FOR 1,000 SOVEREIGNS
W.H.Woolhouse RESPECTFULLY informs his Friends and the Public that the First MATCH of the THREE, between Players of Sussex and the best of ALL ENGLAND, will commence Playing on the New Ground, Darnal, on Whit-Monday. June 4 1827

This was followed by the names of the players, umpires and the 'Gentlemen Backers' for each side. The game would be played between eleven o'clock in the morning and half-past six in the evening. Accommodation would be provided for spectators: 'The Public are respectfully informed, that the Grand Stand is now completed, and presents every accommodation for select parties. Convenient Tents have likewise been erected on the right hand of the Ground, from which an excellent view of the game may be obtained.' Tickets for admission to the grandstand cost a gentleman two shillings and sixpence,[5] the equivalent ladies were charged one shilling, but only if accompanied by a gentleman.

---

5 Around £6.20 in 2010 prices according to the currency converter at www.nationalarchives.gov.uk/currency.

Admission to a tent cost one shilling and sixpence and entrance to the ground only sixpence.

The match started in dramatic fashion. The England team lost their first three wickets in nine balls without scoring a run and then a couple more, including Yorkshire's rising star Tom Marsden, who had scored 227 against Nottingham the year before, for nought with only two runs recorded. The *Sheffield Mercury* reported: 'Such an opening of the game was truly alarming and it was thought that the Fates had conspired against All England. At length the game took a more favourable turn, under the batting of Pilch and Dawson, who sustained the falling cause most manfully.' It seemed that the round-arm bowling of Lillywhite and Broadbridge had been too much for the England batsmen until Fuller arrived at the wicket. He made top score of 38 out of 81, with the *Mercury* reporting: 'Pilch is a powerful young fellow; possessed of muscle and great activity, he has the bat at his complete command. No one could see him without admiring his easy and superior playing. He got his runs principally by four at a stroke.'

Fuller was eventually bowled by Lillywhite in the first innings. Their rivalry would grip the attention of thousands of spectators in all of the games in which they were on opposite sides during their careers. But they were both professionals and there was no animosity between them. In fact, they played together in the same teams on no fewer than 57 occasions.

Sussex won the first of the 'trials' by seven wickets and travelled back south to renew the contest at Lord's twelve days later on 18 and 19 June. Only five of the original All England eleven came down, including William Mathews and Fuller Pilch, who was going to make his second appearance at Lord's seven years after the first. They were joined by three professionals and three MCC members, one of whom was George Knight, the club member who was the driving force behind the idea for the whole series, and was himself a bowler of round-arm, even though in this game and the next he would be in the side confined to bowling under-arm.

Sussex also won the second match, by three wickets, and there were no heroics from Fuller this time. But he was involved in the controversy that threatened to prevent the third and final game taking place. After the match, a statement was issued signed by the eight professionals who had played for All England, plus William Caldecourt the Lord's practice bowler: 'We, the undersigned, do agree that we will not play the third match between All England and Sussex, which is intended to be played at Brighton in July or August, unless the Sussex bowlers bowl fair – that is, abstain from throwing.' The signatories were Thomas Marsden, William Ashby, William Mathews, William Searle, James Saunders, T.C.Howard, W.H. Caldecourt, Fuller Pilch and Thomas Beagley.

This was totally unexpected, bearing in mind that the three games had been set up by MCC for the purpose of testing round-arm bowling at the game's highest level, and it seemed a little odd that they were now

Round-Arm bowling proves its case

THREE GRAND
CRICKET MATCHES,
For 1000 Sovereigns.

The First Match of the Three, between the Players of Sussex and the best of All England, commenced Playing on the New Ground, Darnall, on Whit-Monday Tuesday, and Wednesday, June 4th 5th, & 6th, 1827.

ALL ENGLAND.

First Innings.		Second Innings.	
1 — Flavell	0 bowled by Lillywhite	1 G. E. Dawson	15 bow. by J. Broadbridge
2 — Bowyer	0 hit wicket	2 — Jarvis	17 bowled by do.
3 J. Saunders	0 caught by Slater	3 W. Barber	1 do. by do.
4 W. Barber	1 caught by Dale	4 — Flavell	3 caught by Lillywhite
5 T. Marsden	0 hit wicket	5 F. Pilch	13 caught by Brown
6 G. E. Dawson	13 run out	6 — Jupp	20 caught by Lillywhite
7 F. Pilch	38 bowled by Lillywhite	7 T. Marsden	22 caught by Meads
8 — Matthews	2 ditto by ditto	8 J. Saunders	11 bow. by J. Broadbridge
9 — Beagley	17 ditto by ditto	9 — Beagley.	5 not out
10 — Jarvis	9 c. by J. Broadbridge.	10 — Bowyer	0 bow. by J. Broadbridge
11 — Jupp	0 not out	11 — Matthews	1 bow. by Lillywhite
Byes 1 Total 81		Byes 4 Total 112	

SUSSEX.

First Innings.		Second Innings.	
1 W. Slater	0 caught by Pilch	1 G. Brown	1 caught by Marsden
2 W. Lillywhite	14 stumped by Saunders	2 G. Meads	21 bowled by Pilch
3 Wm. Broadbridge	14 caught by Pilch	3 T. Pierpoint	23 bowled by Marsden
4 J. Twaites	0 caught by Jarvis	4 J. Twaites	37 not out
5 Jas. Broadbridge	0 stumped by Saunders	5 Jas. Broadbridge	15 not out
6 T. Pierpoint	3 caught by Marsden		
7 G. Brown	2 bowled by Matthews	Byes 6	Total 103
8 J. Dale	31 not out		
9 C. Duff.	0 caught by Marsden	Sussex won with 7 wickets to go down	
10 C. Pierpoint	1 bowled by Flavell		
11 G. Meads	26 bowled by Matthews.		
	Total 91		

Umpire for Sussex, Mr. C. ROOTS, of Brighton. Umpire for All England, Mr. JOSEPH DENNIS, of Nottingham.

NAMES OF THE GENTLEMEN BACKERS:—

H. TAMPLIN, Esq. on the part of Sussex; J. JENNER, Esq. on the part of All England.

Every attention will be paid to render the Returns as correct as possible.

T. ORTON, PRINTER, HIGH-STREET, SHEFFIELD.

*Scorecard of the first of three experimental matches.
A thousand sovereigns is the equivalent of £49,500 in 2010 money.*

complaining about the bowling they were being asked by their employers to face. It was rumoured that it was a short-sighted, desperate, last-ditch attempt engineered by a few of the reactionary MCC members to prevent what now seemed to be the inevitable acceptance of the bowling they disliked. By cajoling the players into signing the statement, with either a little sweetener perhaps, or threats of future discrimination when teams were selected for lucrative matches at Lord's, they had hoped to get their own way. Whatever the reason, wiser heads at MCC stepped in and the declaration was eventually withdrawn so the final game could be arranged.

Before they all headed off to Brighton, six of the All England players, Beagley, Searle, Marsden, Saunders, Mathews and Ashby and three of the Sussex professionals, Slater, Thwaites and James Broadbridge, stayed in London to join Caldecourt and Sparks to play against 'Seventeen Gentlemen' at Lord's on 25, 26 and 27 June. In this match the Gentlemen were not banned from using any form of round-arm bowling and George Knight took seven wickets while they dismissed the Players for 128 and 140 to win by 29 runs. Twelve days later Fuller Pilch was back at Lord's with seven others from the All England team to play in a second 'Eleven Players' against 'Seventeen Gentlemen' match on 9, 10 and 11 July. The Gentlemen, including Knight, were on this occasion banned from using any form of round-arm bowling and were thrashed by an innings as the professionals rattled up a massive score of 334, including 100 from Saunders and a useful 38 from Fuller. This was another strong demonstration to those still rejecting round-arm that batting techniques had made so much progress that bowlers had to be allowed to develop their own methods to deal with them.

Five days later, on 16 July, Fuller was again playing at Lord's, this time with the Bury St Edmunds club under the title of Suffolk. There was no organised county cricket structure in those days and for many years clubs would often claim to be representative of their whole county in attempts to add importance to a fixture, sometimes adding well-known guest players as well as their own resident professional, to attract even more paying customers. 'Suffolk' inflicted a memorable defeat of MCC by 22 runs to set up huge expectations for the return at Bury St Edmunds in September.

One week later the final 'experimental' Sussex and All England match began at Brighton on 23 July. *The Times* reported:

> The grand match of cricket, between the county of Sussex and all England, commenced here yesterday. The interest which it had excited is unprecedented, and it is doubtful whether, within the memory of man, so many persons were ever assembled at a cricket-match. People have come, not only from all parts of Sussex, but from London, and even distant parts of England; and the cricketing ground, which is very spacious, and one of the finest in the Kingdom, was literally thronged. The number of spectators present was variously estimated at from 3,000 to 6,000.

It was reported later that the paid attendance at sixpence a head on the first day was 4,480, producing revenue of £112. Even the local military were caught up in the excitement, as *The Times* noted: 'So great was the interest excited respecting this match, that Sir Hussey Vivian, who had fixed an inspection of the 7th Hussars, now lying here, for Monday and Tuesday, changed it to the two preceding days (Saturday and Sunday) for the purpose of enabling an officer of that regiment, Lieutenant Cheslyn, who is on the side of Sussex, to play in the match.'

The home side were strong favourites to win and Lillywhite and Broadbridge appeared unplayable again when All England crashed to 27 all out in their first innings with six noughts in the scorebook. Desperate times called for desperate measures and all restrictions on round-arm bowling were removed so that Knight could finally prove his case on the field and bowl the way he wished. This was a turning point and when Sussex received a taste of their own medicine they were less successful with the bat and All England won by 24 runs.

The visitors could now return to their own counties, while Knight went back to Lord's to continue to argue for a change to the Laws, leaving at least one man in Brighton less than pleased with the result. *The Times* reported: 'There has been a good deal of money lost and won by this match. Lieutenant Cheslyn, of the 7th Hussars, who played on the side of Sussex, had, it is said, lost £300.'

Fuller had made only a handful of runs and taken no wickets at Brighton, but now his presence was needed back at Bury for the Club's most important game in its history on its own ground.

Chapter Six
Bury St Edmunds defeat MCC

There had been rumblings of discontent among other clubs in Suffolk that Bury St Edmunds were calling themselves Suffolk, but picking only their own players. When the match arranged for 27, 28 and 29 August was announced in the *Bury and Norwich Post*, there was an attempt to mollify the critics by indicating that the team to face MCC included players from clubs other than Bury, comprised 'eleven Players of the Ground and the Bury Club and Suffolk.'

The town was in festive mood, according to the *Bury and Norwich Post*, 'preserving the appearance of a full fair day. At an early hour carriages of all descriptions began to arrive with many persons coming from a distance of thirty miles.' Over the three days more than 4,000 spectators paid to watch the game, bringing in revenue of almost £200.

The game lived up to all expectations. Fuller contributed 30 out of Bury's first innings of 115 and took six wickets. After two days, when the betting odds had swung to and fro, Bury needed 60 runs to win on the third morning with six wickets left. Pilch put on 43 with Mr Brand by what the local paper called 'scientific hitting' when he 'was caught by Mr Aislabie, a decision disputed by some of the other Marylebone players. With the scores level and Bury eight wickets down, the next 34 balls were bowled "without a notch" before Bury scraped home on a bye at 7 pm in the evening.'

Fuller received a silver watch and gold chain from a grateful gentleman 'who was a great winner' but cricket was the overall winner, clearly demonstrated by the report in the *Bury and Norwich Post* that 'Mr W.Blake, one of the finest batters, was unfortunate in the first innings and was out on a point of honour which being highly creditable to him as well as illustrative of the friendly manner in which the game was played deserves notice. A ball was bowled to him by Mr G.Knight which he hit at: the wicket-keeper, Dark, who appealed to the umpire if it were out. The umpire decided it was not out. Mr Blake stated that it was impossible for the umpire to be aware of the circumstances, but the ball did touch his fingernail consequently it was a catch and he should go out.' Perfectly appropriate for a gentleman of any team in the nineteenth century, of course. In the light of the modern practice where batsmen have almost completely banished the practice of 'walking' back to the pavilion without waiting for the umpire's decision, it would be interesting to know if the professionals of those days would have been just as honest as Mr Blake of Bury. And honest or not, Fuller and the other professionals were not allowed to enjoy the benefits of their success at the end of each day as extravagantly as the 'Gentlemen of the Clubs' who, according to the press, 'went to dinner at the Angel Inn to partake of a turtle weighing 100 lbs, two fine haunches of venison, and five salmon contributed by one of the members of the Bury Club.'

In 1828 Bury again assumed the title of Suffolk when they went to Lord's to play MCC on 9 and 10 June, although they were unable to repeat their success of the previous year, losing by 24 runs. Fuller top-scored in their first innings with 44 out of 96 and took some wickets but it was not enough. A few days later a letter appeared in the *Suffolk Chronicle* complaining that Bury had no right to call themselves Suffolk as there were no players in the side from other villages in the county. Pilch was not mentioned by name but there was objection to the presence in the team of an outsider who was 'formerly a celebrated player at Holt in Norfolk but was hired and has been supported for four or five years by the Bury Club.'

Charles Leech, local solicitor and the man largely responsible for raising the Bury Club to 'the marked eminence it now possesses', dismissed the objections and insisted that Bury was the only club in the county who could afford the expense of playing MCC, and without hired players, Suffolk would be unable to compete at that level.

Two weeks later Fuller Pilch was asked to play at Lord's on 24 and 25 June in the first of two 'special' matches set up by MCC, starting with England against 'The Bs', a strong team made up from players whose surname began with that letter, including the fast round-arm specialist James Broadbridge. After this game, Fuller travelled north where he was employed to play for Leicester against Sheffield in Leicester on 30 June and 1 July, and then in the return at Sheffield on 7, 8, 9 and 10 July. Leicester won both games despite the efforts of Marsden, who scored 145 runs for Sheffield from his four innings; these, though, could not compare to a good all-round performance from Fuller who took 15 wickets as well as scoring 78 runs in his three innings. Fuller would go back to Sheffield in September but first he returned to Lord's on 14, 15 and 16 July to play in a Right-Handed *v* Left-Handed match, the first since 1790. Then he was selected to play for England against Sussex at Brighton on 21, 22 and 23 July, where he faced Lillywhite for the only time that season and was bowled by him without scoring in the second innings, having only made seven in the first.

The following week, in the return match at Bury against MCC, on 28, 29 and 30 July, the home side played as Bury not Suffolk, despite the earlier arguments put forward by Charles Leech, and won by 12 runs. Fuller proved his importance to the team by top-scoring in both innings, 28 out of 57 and 43 out of 108, as well as bowling down nine wickets. These were the only two matches where Fuller turned out for Bury that summer, missing both matches home and away to Norwich; and it seems as if he had outgrown the Club, and had started to explore other options.

The match at Sheffield on 8, 9 and 10 September had originated in a challenge to the rest of England from William Woolhouse, proprietor of the Darnall ground. To make the affair even more attractive to paying customers, the Sheffield side was converted into 'Three Counties' and incorporated players from Nottingham, Leicester as well as Sheffield, so that it became an early version of North v South. As expected, large crowds gathered to watch and it was reported in the *Sheffield Chronicle* that, on the second day, 'several ladies also contributed by their presence to enliven the scene', perhaps the nineteenth century equivalent of the T20 cheerleaders of today. Despite his previous outings for Leicester, Fuller was engaged to play for England and the cocky northerners were put in their place by the cream of southern England's cricketers who won by an enormous 242 runs, thanks to the round-arm bowling of Lillywhite taking twelve wickets and Broadbridge taking seven, with one run out. On the batting side Fuller excelled by top scoring in both innings with 49 and 56, his second innings described by the *Chronicle* as: 'Pilch again made a tremendous innings, several bowlers were tried but all to no purpose. Rawlins bowled a few overs. In one of them, Pilch got three four strokes, which excited a murmur against Rawlins, while all admired the ease which the batsman displayed.'

Seeking to cash in on the South's victory in the north, Charles Leech gave an indication of how much the Bury Club valued the services of Fuller Pilch by issuing a challenge on his behalf to Thomas Marsden of Sheffield to a single wicket contest, for £50 or £100 a game. Naturally the Yorkshireman was interested but Fuller did not feel ready for the challenge and it would be another five years before the contest took place when, due to further successes of both batsmen, it would be for the title 'Champion of England'.

Chapter Seven
Committed to East Anglia, for now

The Bury Club agreed in 1829 that Fuller Pilch could play more frequently for Norfolk, the county of his birth, and developed closer links with the Club in Norwich. But as his fame spread he became the player the public wanted to see and all 'gentlemen cricketers' wanted to play with or against, and it was not long before Surrey and Kent came calling with attractive offers.

His season had started unsuccessfully at Lord's, first in the Married v Single match on 1 and 2 June and then three weeks later playing for the Players against the Gentlemen, where MCC were determined to reverse the usual result and make the game more competitive by employing two professionals, Lillywhite and Broadbridge, to strengthen the bowling for the Gentlemen. Fuller went for his first pair, out for nought twice to the fast round-arm bowling of Broadbridge.

It is a credit to Fuller's dedication that he was able to concentrate on the match in hand when frequently finding himself playing against new opponents one day and a week later joining them to play another team somewhere else. From 2 July until 7 August, Fuller played in six matches in five weeks, starting at Lord's with Norfolk against MCC when he made a major contribution to his county's victory by scoring an unbeaten 38 of the first innings total of 56. He then switched sides to play two games almost back-to-back for Suffolk against Norfolk. In the first, completed in one day on 13 July, he made 37 not out of Suffolk's first innings 59 at Norwich but it was not enough to prevent a Norfolk victory by 17 runs. Suffolk won the return at Bury St Edmunds on 23 and 24 July and then went down to Lord's to beat MCC by 15 runs on 27, 28 and 29 July. For the annual match between Bury and MCC on 3, 4 and 5 August, when the stakes had risen to 1,000 guineas, MCC decided to come to Bury strengthened by two professionals, Saunders and Searle. But it made no difference as Fuller top-scored in both Bury innings, 42 out of 111 in the first and 13 out of 66 in the second, and Bury won by 19 runs. The next day, five of the MCC team who had played against Bury went with Fuller to play with him for Norfolk at Dereham against a revised MCC team. Again Fuller top-scored in both innings with 30 out of 95 and an unbeaten 15 out of 48 while steering Norfolk to a six-wicket victory. During this marathon Fuller was on the winning side in five out of the six low-scoring games, contributing 237 runs out of the 804 runs made by whichever of the teams he was playing for, more than 30 per cent, and top scoring in seven of the twelve innings, although he never reached a half-century.

Taking a brief respite from his responsibilities in East Anglia, Fuller travelled down to Brighton to play for England against Sussex on 17, 18 and 19 August and was dismissed twice by William Lillywhite, after making 18 in the first innings but without scoring in the second. Then he returned to Suffolk to appear for Bury against Woodbridge on 25 and 26 August before hurrying off to Godalming to play for England against Surrey the next day where he faced Lillywhite and Broadbridge again as given men for the county. His last appearance of the season was for Bury at Woodbridge in the return match on 14 and 15 September.

The 1830 season was very much more of the same for Fuller, with appearances for eight different teams including three games for Bury, two for Norfolk, and one appearance for Suffolk at Lord's. He began by joining the Bury team at Woodbridge on 10 June where his 38 out of 56 in Bury's second innings ensured victory by 23 runs. A few days later Fuller arrived in London for a series of four consecutive matches at Lord's. The annual Gentlemen v Players match starting on 14 June was rained off before Fuller could have a turn at the wicket. This time he was supporting the Gentlemen after being engaged, with Lillywhite, to appear against the professionals in another attempt to balance the strength of the two sides and make the result less predictable. The weather improved and Fuller joined a Suffolk side strengthened by Searle, Broadbridge and Beagley playing an MCC eleven that also included three given men, Marsden, Lillywhite and Saunders, on 21 and 22 June. Fuller played an outstanding innings when, in reply to MCC's 117,[6] he ensured Suffolk stayed in the game with a first innings lead of 29 while he remained unbeaten on 70. The *Suffolk Chronicle* reported that 'the batting of Pilch on Monday evening for more than 3 hours and the following day for 2 hours without giving a single chance to his formidable opponents was never before surpassed.' The result was touch and go with the visitors needing 28 to win and losing five wickets until Fuller hit the winning shot, ensuring that he remained unbeaten in either innings by Lillywhite. This was his last appearance for Suffolk and he ended with a career record for the county of 315 runs from seven matches with an average of 28.64, plus 34 wickets.

On 28 and 29 June, Fuller was engaged to appear at Lord's for the Gentlemen of England against the Gentlemen of Hampshire team strengthened by the bowling of Broadbridge, who bowled him for nought in the first innings, and Lillywhite, who dismissed him for seven in the second, before the Gentlemen of England won by seven wickets. Neither of them, playing for MCC against Norfolk, could get him out at Lord's a week later where his 28 out of 58 in the county's second innings ensured victory by 24 runs.

The month of July also saw the first attempt by a club to lure Fuller south of the Thames on a permanent basis when he was hired by Surrey to play

---

6   He took five wickets in this innings, the first occasion where he is known to have done this in a recognised first-class match.

twice against Sussex, the first-ever matches between those two counties. The first was at Godalming in Surrey on 8 and 9 July when Fuller impressed with scores of 24 and 26 as well as bowling down six wickets to help Surrey win by 197 runs. This was followed by another appearance at Lord's on 12, 13 and 14 July, where MCC had decided to put on a revised version of Gentlemen *v* Players, but this time as an all-Gentlemen match with five professional engaged for one side including Fuller, and four for the other, including Lillywhite. The experiment did produce a closer game for once, with victory for the Six Gentlemen and Five Players. Then it was time for the second game for Surrey away to Sussex at Midhurst on 16 and 17 July, where Fuller gave Surrey a good start with a top score of 27 in their first innings and took four wickets in a match that ended unfinished due to rain.

Fuller went back to Suffolk to play for Bury in the return match with Woodbridge on 22 and 23 July where he recorded the first hundred of his career, making 127 not out. This significant event was described in *Scores and Biographies*: 'Though this was not a first-rate match, still it must be observed that Fuller Pilch's runs were made against Mathews [one of the best bowlers of the day], W.Pilch, and Caldecourt.' Then the attractions of Kent beckoned and back down south he went to take advantage of an engagement offered by the Town Malling club to play in two matches against Benenden.

Twelve months earlier, a group of tradesmen had met at the George Inn in West Malling, a small market town near Maidstone, and formed a cricket team to rival an existing team known as 'The Gentlemen of Malling' which had been established the year before by Thomas Selby, a local solicitor. After a series of matches between the two rival teams, they were amalgamated to play in future as 'Town Malling', at the New Cricket Ground. The Benenden team had been in existence for some years before that and were now backed by Thomas Law Hodges, son of the High Sheriff of Kent. Hodges had plans that the club would eventually play on the family estate in Hemsted Park, near Benenden, but the first game was on the village green at Benenden on 30 and 31 July and ended unfinished. Both clubs were obviously ambitious but it was Thomas Selby who had come up with the idea of bringing two famous professionals, Pilch and Broadbridge, to his club that summer. It certainly paid off for Town Malling as more than 8,000 spectators turned up on 6 August for the one-day return match that was also left unfinished, even though it started at 9 am. Entrance was free but no doubt the local tradesmen made the most of their opportunity. Fuller did not exactly rise to the occasion, scoring only 26 runs during his four visits to the wicket and taking six wickets overall. Broadbridge fared better with 14 victims and top score in Town Malling's first innings at Benenden with an unbeaten 23 out of 60.

Fuller ended his summer playing in East Anglia. First, at Bury St Edmunds against MCC on 16 and 17 August, with each team strengthened by five professionals, he made 34 out of Bury's first innings total of 74, but it was not enough to prevent victory for MCC by 12 runs. It was a different story at Dereham on 19 and 20 August where he helped Norfolk beat an even stronger MCC side by eight wickets.

First-hand experience of the attractions south of the Thames appear to have made Fuller more aware than ever of his close family ties to Norfolk. In 1831, now 27, he moved to Norwich as the club professional and lessee of the cricket ground, with assistance from brother William. He also took over as proprietor of a nearby inn and pleasure gardens on Bracondale Hill. Right at the start of the season in May he was welcomed back to the county by his brother Nathaniel to play in the Brinton village team in home and away matches against the village team of Litcham which included their other brother William and players from Brisley switching sides after each game. Fuller made 32 out of 73 in Brinton's first innings in the first game on 18 May and an unbeaten 41 out of 58 in Brinton's first innings in the second on 29 May. Showing no respect for the celebrity status of his younger brother, William clean bowled Fuller in three of his four innings and Litcham won both games.

Fuller spent much of June, July and the first week of August in London where he took part in six consecutive matches at Lord's. All three Pilch brothers represented the Norwich club at Lord's on 6, 7 and 8 June. After Fuller had top-scored with 65 out of 142 in their second innings to set MCC a target of 113, Norwich won by 45 runs with William taking six wickets. Then Fuller played in the England eleven against a team formed from players with surnames beginning with the letter 'B' again. It was a two-day match arranged for 13 and 14 June, but ended on the first after the 'Bs' were dismissed for 18 and 35, with only Beagley reaching double figures, in reply to 81. One week later he was once more engaged by Surrey to play, and lose, against England on 21 and 22 June: he then joined the Bury club at Lord's to play MCC on 27 and 28 June where his 44 out of 66 in the first innings kept Bury in the match but with the home club running out winners by 68 runs. A week later Norfolk arrived in the capital to lose by seven wickets to MCC on 4 and 5 July, after Fuller's major contribution of 28 in the second innings of 113 had appeared to give the county a fighting chance. On 24 and 25 July, MCC came up with another original idea in their usual attempt to make the Gentlemen v Players match more competitive. They reduced the size of the Players team to only nine, including Fuller Pilch, against a full eleven of Gentlemen. It made no difference and the Players won by five wickets with Fuller in the middle when the winning stroke was made. The following week Fuller and Lillywhite were 'given men' for MCC on 2 and 3 August, against a strong England eleven that won by an innings.

If there were any engagements on offer from clubs in Kent during this period, Fuller had ignored them and now the season at Lord's was over he returned to Norfolk and Suffolk to face an MCC touring team strengthened by Lillywhite, Wenman and Saunders. Norwich faced the tourists first at Norwich on 8, 9 and 10 August, where William Pilch's 21 out of 69 in the first innings and Fuller's 47 out of 91 in the second still left them short by

38 runs. The following day, at Dereham, it was Norfolk's turn to face MCC and lose by 69 runs after the county had been dismissed for only eleven runs in the first innings with no batsman reaching double figures and Lillywhite taking nine wickets. They managed to make 38 in the second innings with no-one into double figures again except Fuller with 13.

Fuller had not completely severed his connections with Bury and played his last game for them against the same MCC touring team on 15 and 16 August. But the Suffolk club was again easily beaten and their glory days seemed to be coming to an end. Fuller's career record for Bury was exceptional with 1,155 runs from 26 appearances with an average of 28.17, plus 102 wickets. Fuller returned to Brinton on 7 September for their third and final match with Litcham when his unbeaten 96 gave them revenge for their earlier defeat.

Chapter Eight
A year of indecision

In 1832 Fuller Pilch abandoned Norfolk and Suffolk and went in search of pastures new. He spent the summer travelling between Cambridge, London and Kent, exploring the options open to him as a professional cricketer for hire.

He first linked up with William Caldecourt at Cambridge, where the experienced practice bowler from Lord's (where he had been employed since 1818) frequently spent the spring as coach to the undergraduates. William Glover, in *Memoirs of a Cambridge Chorister*, originally published in 1885, remembered watching Fuller at coaching sessions: 'It was delightful to witness Pilch's demeanour, even on practice days. I never saw instruction of any kind so conveyed, or so received. His words were few and simple, yet always to the purpose. A gentle hint on this point, a gesture on that, and all given with a patient smile of conscious power certain to be recognised by his admiring auditors.'

Fuller began his season at Lord's on 25 and 26 June, for England against Sussex. His unbeaten 40 in England's second innings saw them through to a five-wicket victory. The following week Fuller and Caldecourt played as given men for Cambridgeshire beating MCC at Lord's by six wickets on 2 and 3 July. Caldecourt bowled down seven wickets in the match and Fuller had six as well as making 50 out of 103 in the Cambridgeshire first innings and an unbeaten 41 in the second. Then Thomas Selby attracted Fuller back into the Town Malling team to play home and away games against the combined villages of Leeds and Bearsted, the first at Leeds Park near Maidstone on 25 and 26 July, where he met Alfred Mynn for the first time. Neither bowled the other out and Fuller top-scored in both innings with 13 and 20 to see Town Malling to victory. At George Field in Town Malling, for the return six days later, they met again and after the visitors had been dismissed for 45 Town Malling rattled up 112 for the loss of one wicket leaving Fuller unbeaten on 72; Leeds and Bearsted were thus persuaded to give up the match at the end of the first day. Fuller stayed in Kent and the next stop was Dartford Brent on 6 August where, this time, Fuller played for Leeds against a much stronger Dartford who had engaged three professionals and won by an innings. One week later Fuller was playing at Chislehurst with Lillywhite for MCC against the Gentlemen of Kent, where the combination of their round-arm and under-arm bowling was not enough to stave off defeat by three wickets.

On 20 and 21 August, Fuller and Caldecourt were back at Cambridge again to appear as given men for Cambridgeshire at Chatteris against MCC, 'in the presence of an immense assemblage of spectators from the surrounding parts,' according to the *Cambridge Independent Press*. Cambridgeshire repeated their earlier victory, thanks to Fuller's top score of 28 out of 78 and taking six wickets. Two days later Fuller and Caldecourt played for Cambridge Town against MCC on Parker's Piece in Cambridge and enjoyed a third victory.

Fuller went back to Lord's for the Gentlemen v Players challenge on 27 and 28 August when, in another unsuccessful attempt to make the game more competitive, the Gentlemen defended the smaller-size wicket that had been in use fifty years earlier before the MCC amended the Laws. This was Alfred Mynn's first match at Lord's and, although he could not prevent a Players' victory by an innings and 34 runs, he did get Fuller out caught for only eleven runs. Two days later Fuller met Mynn again, but this time he was co-opted to join him in an attempt to strengthen the Leeds and Bearsted team against the powerful Dartford eleven, but they did not have enough time to finish the game which ended with Dartford seven wickets down but still eight runs short. Fuller remained in Kent for his last game of the summer when he went back to Chislehurst on 10 and 11 September to play in a twelve-a-side match between the Gentlemen of England plus Pilch, Lillywhite and Cobbett, against the Gentlemen of Kent, including Mynn and three professionals. Fuller top-scored with 32 out of 76 in the Gentlemen of England side's first innings but the Gentlemen of Kent won by nine runs. Mynn did not take Fuller's wicket as a bowler this time, but he did catch him in the second innings, probably in the slips, where Mynn was renowned for having a safe pair of hands, although Fuller believed he 'didn't need both' and declared in 'The Game of Cricket': 'one hand was good enough for Alfred, for his fist was about the size of a small shoulder of mutton.'

Chapter Nine
Champion of England, Part One

Arrangements for a single-wicket challenge were eventually agreed by Thomas Marsden and Fuller Pilch by the start of the 1833 season. The first of the two encounters would be held at Norwich on 18 July, so it seems that, for the time being, a future in Kent had been rejected by Fuller. In fact, on 25 June, the day before he was supposed to be playing for Town Malling at Tunbridge Wells, he was in Norfolk playing for Norwich against Brinton. Two weeks earlier he had started his season at Lord's on 10 June, playing in an A-K *v* L-Z match, where he took seven wickets in his opponents' first innings, his best return in first-class cricket. (At this stage of his career he was almost an all-rounder.) A week later he joined William Lillywhite as a pair of given men in an MCC team at Lord's against the Gentlemen of Kent, where he was bowled by Mynn in both innings. After the match at Norwich he was back at Lord's on 1 and 2 July in the England eleven against Sussex. Fuller had only managed 56 runs from eight innings in those four matches so he joined his brothers Nathaniel and William in a Norwich eleven against the Rest of Norfolk on 4 July and took the opportunity for some extra batting practice while scoring an unbeaten 115.

So now Fuller was ready for his big test. His challenger, Thomas Marsden, was at the peak of his career and carried the hopes and ambitions of Sheffield and all Yorkshire on his shoulders:

> O, Marsden at cricket is nature's perfection
> For hitting the ball in any direction;
> He ne'er fears his wicket, so safely he strikes,
> And he does with the bat and ball as he likes.
> *A Cricket Song, Scores and Biographies, Volume 1*

Only one year younger than Fuller, Marsden was a left-handed, 'tremendous hard slashing' batsman and a left-handed, fast under-hand bowler, occasionally changing to medium-pace round-arm. He is first recorded playing for Sheffield in 1824 where he remained for the whole of his career. Marsden first met Fuller in 1827 when they were selected to play for the England team that faced Sussex in the three round-arm 'trial' matches. They also played together on six other occasions between 1828 and 1832, four times in the Gentlemen *v* Players matches at Lord's, and twice more for an England team against Sussex at Brighton. The first time they were on opposite sides was in 1828 when Fuller went north to play twice for Leicester against Sheffield, and later that year they met again at Lord's in the Right-Handed *v* Left-Handed match. Pilch and Marsden were famously pitted against each other in both the Bury St Edmunds *v* MCC matches in 1830, with Fuller outshining his future challenger. The next summer, at Lord's, playing for England against an MCC side that included Fuller, Marsden was more successful and helped England win by an innings. Marsden did not take many wickets in any of these encounters, nor did he ever dismiss Fuller, so his bowling appeared to present no problems for the Norfolk man. But the same could be said for the bowling of Fuller as he is only recorded as bowling Marsden out once.

Marsden certainly had more experience of single-wicket cricket, a version of the game that Fuller had avoided as often as possible. According to the *Norwich Mercury*:

> For years past Marsden has stood forward as the challenger of any man in England at single wicket, and his success in the West, as well as the exhibition of some excellent play at various times in London, appears to have given many good judges an opinion that at this particular game he has no equal.

But others had been less impressed. Pierce Egan's *Book of Sports* suggested in a poem 'The Cricket Eleven of England' that the talents of Marsden were less than his local supporters believed:

> Next Marsden may come, th'it here must be stated
> That his skill down at Sheffield is oft over-rated.

There was no clear favourite. The *Norwich Mercury* reported: 'Opinion was perhaps never so much divided amongst the avowed judges and patrons of the game as upon this match. We understand that at Lord's Ground 5 to 4 has been betted on each champion, and on our own ground, before the match commenced we believe odds were laid both ways'.

They were going to meet under single-wicket Laws which applied to just two players with no fieldsmen to assist them and batting for two innings each. Runs could only be scored from hits forward beyond a line marked at right angles extending 22 yards on either side of the single set of stumps, known as the 'bounds'. When making a scoring hit the batsman had to have one of his feet on the ground behind the popping crease. To qualify as one run the batsman had to run and touch the single stump at the bowler's end and return safely back to his own area. There was no wicket-keeper, so no runs could be made from byes, leg-byes or overthrows. Both men had to be extremely fit to face the prospect of spending a whole day fielding to their own bowling and, when batting, having to run two lengths of the pitch to score any runs. A quick single was going to have to be very quick indeed.

Marsden won the toss and decided to bat first. Play began at mid-day and after 41 balls from Fuller he had scored seven runs from 33 hits in 36 minutes before being bowled. Fuller went in at 1 pm and Marsden began bowling fast under-arm. Despite changing to round-arm, or what the press called 'the modern throwing style', Fuller had reached 74 not out by 3 pm from 110 hits to 128 balls. The *Norwich Mercury* reported that 'Pilch made fearless and destructive havoc with almost all that were delivered to him.'

An interval was taken for 'dinner'. Fuller hit three runs from the first ball after play restarted at 4.25 pm, and one wonders what he had just eaten to give him the strength and energy to strike the ball far enough away from Marsden to be able to run six lengths of the pitch while the bowler pursued and returned the ball. But two balls later a ball struck Fuller on the leg and went on to his stumps.

Marsden's second innings started at 5 pm and he played seven balls without scoring before lifting the ball up into the hands of Fuller for an easy catch. Marsden's efforts were summed up succinctly in the *Norwich Mercury* as: 'it appeared to us that he was no match for Pilch; he could not get his balls away.' The challenge had been expected to take at least two, if not three, days. The *Mercury* commented: 'There is only one point that gives cause for regret; it is that Fuller Pilch, in spite of his victory, is likely to be a considerable loser, arising from the short time the game lasted. This however we hope will be in some way lightened, as at the moment we go to press a most capital double wicket match is going on upon the ground.' The two teams included both Fuller and Marsden, plus the two umpires Caldecourt and Dark, the promoter of the return challenge at Sheffield, Woolhouse, and the Pilch brothers, Nathaniel and William. The scorecard for this impromptu game was not recorded.

Chapter Ten
Champion of England, Part Two

The second part of the challenge was played at Sheffield two weeks later and advertised in the *Sheffield Mercury*:

Hyde Park Cricket Ground
GREAT SINGLE CRICKET MATCH FOR £100
W.Woolhouse respectfully informs his friends and the Public that the GREAT SINGLE CRICKET MATCH, between MARSDEN and PILCH, will commence playing on Monday, August 5th, 1833. Stumps to be pitched at one o'clock
Umpires, Messrs J.Dark and W.Caldecourt, from Lord's Cricket Ground, London
Admittance to the Ground 6d; to the Stand 1s
NB No Dogs allowed on the Ground'

Batting first this time, Fuller played much more cautiously and occupied the crease for nearly five hours while scoring 82 runs from 198 balls, including four wides. At the end of the day Marsden was unbeaten on 26 and it was beginning to look that this time, in front of his own supporters, he was going to make it a genuine contest. But it was not to be: he was bowled without adding to his total at the start of the second day. According to the *Sheffield Independent*, Pilch then 'commenced his second innings with his accustomed coolness, and played with as much ease and as little embarrassment as possible.' Play ended for the day when he was bowled for 100 from 148 hits facing 200 balls plus six wides. Needing 162 runs to win, Marsden made a real fight of it and by dinner on the third day he was 35 not out after facing 183 balls. Of the resumption of play, the *Independent* reported that 'Marsden again took his bat, when a most tremendous ball was delivered by Pilch, which put an end to one of greatest and most important matches ever played.' The *Independent* summed it up: 'The batting of Pilch was of the most superior description; in fact he may be considered the crack player of England. The grace, ease, and certainty with which he met the best of Marsden's balls, excited universal astonishment and praise.'

Five days after the second single-wicket challenge, Fuller and Marsden were at Chislehurst playing for MCC against the Gentlemen of Kent. It seems that there was no ill-feeling between the two Championship contenders and they may even have been on the same stagecoach to travel south together for the first of a short series of matches in which they would be joining forces. For Fuller it was very much a question of the 'glorious uncertainty of cricket' when he was out for a 'pair' at Chislehurst, although in a second single-innings game, got up when the first finished early, he did manage to score 10 before being bowled by Mynn. Then it was on to Brighton to play for England against Sussex on 19 and 20 August. Just over a week later Fuller was back in Sheffield, at the Hyde Park ground, with his two brothers to play for Norfolk against Yorkshire, a match eagerly awaited by the *Sheffield Independent*:

> Nothing can exceed the interest this match excites in Sheffield and its neighbourhood, and many hundreds are betted upon the event, Norfolk for choice in consequence of the three Pilch's, who are reckoned first raters, playing on that side. The Yorkshire players, likewise, have got a tower of strength in their eleven, the best perhaps, that ever turned out upon the field. Many improvements have been made on the ground, and a large tent, which will accommodate nearly 200 persons, has been erected for the gentlemen subscribers and their friends.

All eyes were on the new Champion. The *Independent* reported that 'when the great gun of the south, Fuller Pilch, took his bat, a buzz of expectation ran around the ring. His batting was very fine, but an unlucky ball was cleverly caught by Vincent, who was "wide awake" and ready for anything.'

Marsden top-scored in his county's second innings with 53 before Fuller bowled him and Norfolk needed 268 to win. Wickets fell quickly, though and the *Independent* reported:

> Fuller Pilch came next, and, with his brother, remained at the wicket a considerable time. The batting of the two brothers was a rich treat to the amateurs. Dearman bowled with wonderful swiftness, and, about five o'clock a queer ball left Nathaniel Pilch minus two stumps. Fuller still played on, but Vincent was behind him. A ball bounded from his bat over his shoulder and his backer at once relieved him from all further labour.

Norfolk collapsed for 147 all out, so that Yorkshire won by 120 runs. The *Independent* commented: 'Thus ended this interesting match contrary to the expectations of the knowing ones, who reckoned that the Pilch's would carry all before them. Marsden's playing was such as to convince the amateurs that he has no equal in a full field.' It added that 'Though at single wicket, Fuller Pilch, from his greater length, has the advantage, yet his practice for single wicket is a disadvantage to him in a game like this.'

The three brothers went back to Norfolk to resume their rivalry, appearing on different sides of a Brinton match at home to Norwich on 13 September that also featured William Pilch junior, making his first appearance alongside Uncle Fuller.

Despite the discomfort of more lengthy rides by stagecoach from one end of the country to the other, an unavoidable price to pay by professional cricketers in those times if they wished to maintain their reputations, Fuller and Marsden were soon back in Brighton for another match against

Print of Fuller Pilch, from The Cricket Field, probably made in the 1840s, but showing him as a rather younger man. He is keeping his legs out of the way, though perhaps he has 'modern-style' shin pads under his trousers. Unspliced bats were still common at this time.

Sussex on 17 and 18 September. Fuller top-scored with 34 out of England's first innings total of 95 and they went on to their third victory over Sussex that season. That was enough for Fuller and his season was over, but Marsden went straight back to Yorkshire to play one last game for Sheffield against a twenty-two of Bedale.

Chapter Eleven
Norfolk: the final years

The 1834 season was a vintage year for Fuller Pilch with two centuries in important matches and four half-centuries. He spent the first two months of the summer in Norfolk playing in club matches with his brothers and nephew, scoring 170 runs in his five innings in preparation for the arrival on 18 June of a representative team from Yorkshire for a county match. Although there was some criticism that as nearly all their players were from Sheffield it did not represent the county it was announced in posters throughout Norwich as: 'The Great Match of Cricket between Yorkshire and Norfolk will take place at Norwich on Wednesday, 18th June 1834 and following days. The Match will include the celebrated Marsden and Dearman, The Three Pilches, and the best players of the two counties.'

Norfolk batted first: the *Norfolk Chronicle* reported that 'Fuller Pilch went in fourth and shewed himself a perfect master of the science, notwithstanding he had most experienced bowling against him he held his bat to the end of the day, when the Norfolk side had scored 175, with four wickets to go down. On the following morning (Thursday) the game was resumed, and the Norfolk men raised their innings to 215, Fuller Pilch carrying out his bat.' With 87 runs Fuller must have been disappointed that he had not reached the coveted three figures, and after Yorkshire had been skittled out for 37, set about making amends in his second innings before falling short again with 73. The day ended with Norfolk 155 for three and eventually Yorkshire were asked to make a colossal 369 to win. Then William Pilch got among the Yorkshire batsman taking six wickets, either caught or bowled, another huge Pilch family contribution to a win by 272 runs.

It was then down to London for England against Sussex on 2 and 3 July, where Fuller made his first century at Lord's (and his first in what we now regard as first-class cricket), 105 not out, after retiring hurt for a short time having been hit by the ball on the brow of his left eye, then returning in style: 'After a few runs he began to feel his bat and fours, fives, sixes and even a seven were scored.' Not even Lillywhite, who took 11 wickets in the match, could hold him back.

Four days later Kent came to Lord's for the first match they had played as a county for over five years and the first England versus Kent match on level terms since the eighteenth century. But Kent now had Alfred Mynn in their ranks for the first time and, although he could not save them from defeat after Kent were dismissed for 21 on the first day, he bowled Fuller for only

43

THE

GREAT MATCH

OF CRICKET

BETWEEN

YORKSHIRE & NORFOLK,

WILL TAKE PLACE AT NORWICH,

ON

WEDNESDAY, 18th JUNE, 1834,

AND FOLLOWING DAYS

THE MATCH WILL INCLUDE THE

CELEBRATED MARSDEN & DEARMAN,

THE THREE PILCHES,

AND THE BEST PLAYERS OF THE TWO COUNTIES

Handbill for the Norfolk v Yorkshire match played at Norwich in 1834. The home side included the brothers Fuller, Nathaniel and William Pilch, and won by 272 runs. Fuller himself scored 87 and 73.

two in the England first innings when great things had been expected from the Norfolk man.

A week later Fuller joined his brothers in Sheffield for Norfolk's return match with Yorkshire at the Hyde Park ground. Starting on 14 July this would end in controversy after five days in which play was seriously reduced by rain. Yorkshire started well with 191 and then dismissed Norfolk for 75 despite strong resistance from William Pilch who scored 30. A massive 296 from Yorkshire in their second innings left Norfolk needing 413 to win, a seemingly impossible task when Fuller went to the wicket at 1 pm on the fourth day. However, when rain put an end to play on the Friday he was still there with an unbroken 153 after what the *Sheffield Independent* praised as 'batting ... most beautiful, and proves him the finest player in the country.' But the Norfolk players could not afford to stay another night in their lodgings and their 'sponsor', Squire Rippingall, was not prepared to put his hand in his pocket to help. According to the *Independent*, the match was 'given up in favour of Sheffield and the stakes handed over as the three players to go in were some of the worst bats of their party.'[7] They had no chance of winning.' Although Norfolk still needed another 124 to win, the *Norfolk Chronicle* did not agree and believed that, with three wickets in hand and Fuller still there, Norfolk might have won, 'had there been means of playing it out.' Fuller's 153 not out was his highest score in matches now assessed by the ACS as 'first-class'; a picture of him from about this time shows him holding a plain, 'unspliced' bat. It helped him to a season's first-class aggregate of 551 runs at 61.22; the season's second-highest run scorer, Thomas Marsden, totalled just 156.

Returning to the south, Fuller renewed his relationship with Town Malling on 25 July and played as a given man at home to Chislehurst and Bromley. Then it was up to Lord's for the Gentlemen *v* Players game on 28 and 29 July, won easily as usual by the Players thanks to an innings of 60 from Fuller before being bowled by Mynn. On 12 August he joined the England team at Chislehurst for a match against Kent and when the match finished early he even had time to relax and enjoy an impromptu, three-sided single-wicket challenge of one innings with Marsden, Lillywhite, Mynn, Wenman and Mills. It seems that the attractions of Kent were becoming more and more irresistible.

On 18 August Fuller arrived in Brighton to join the England team, less Lillywhite and Box who changed sides to play for their county, in the return match with Sussex that ended after two days with another defeat for the county. Then he returned to Bromley on 22 August to appear for Town Malling, who were, no doubt, delighted to have him back for their game away to Chislehurst and Bromley as his 49 out of 94 in Town Malling's first innings played a major part in their victory by 82 runs. Fuller's season

---

[7] The three players concerned – Laws, Englebright and Howard – had scored two runs between them in the first innings, with the last of these dismissed hit-wicket. It was not until 1896 that a side scored more than 400 runs in the fourth innings of a first-class match.

seems to have ended early, as there is no record of him playing again in 1834.

The decision to move south was finally made in August 1835. But the year started for Fuller with a few weeks at Cambridge helping his old friend Caldecourt to coach the University undergraduates, including an exhibition three-a-side, single-wicket challenge on 2 June for which they were joined by Redgate, Fenner, Saunders and Parnther, described in *Bell's Life* as 'truly the finest display of cricketing skills ever witnessed on Parker's Piece.' This was the first time that Fuller faced Sam Redgate, the 24-year-old round-arm bowler from Nottingham, whose bowling was described by Haygarth as 'very fast and ripping, with a good deal of "spin"'. Fuller struggled against him in the first innings, managing only four hits from seven balls before being bowled without scoring. In the second innings Fuller, going in last and needing 32 runs to win, took his time to study Redgate's venomous bowling and managed to hit 39 of the 57 balls he faced but had only scored six runs before Redgate bowled his wicket down for the second time.

A brief return to Norfolk followed, for a couple of club matches, and then Fuller bid farewell to his family and headed south to Hemsted Park in Kent where Thomas Hodges and his son had now established their cricket ground for the village team of Benenden and were due to face Kent on 2 and 3 July. The ground was encircled by marquees and accommodated over 5,000 spectators. 'The new ground and the fine scenery about this enchanting spot won the admiration of everyone' and Kent brought a strong team that included Alfred Mynn. As a 'given' man for Benenden, Fuller top-scored in both innings with 25 out of 74 and 33 out of 120, but this could not prevent a Kent victory by three wickets.

It was unlikely that the Hodges were thinking of offering a permanent position to Fuller, whereas the consortium at Town Malling of Thomas Selby, Silas Norton and Lord Harris had been formed with the aim of promoting county cricket in the George Field at West Malling, despite being little more than a village with just two main streets and barely 1,500 residents. They now convinced Fuller to settle in the town in return for a salary of £100 a year,[8] and the position as landlord of the George tavern. The average annual earnings of a farm worker in 1835 was £40, a skilled industrial worker between £60 and £70, and a teacher £82, so Fuller was doing well, and of course still able to augment his income by accepting engagements for other teams at about £5 a match. Despite his celebrity, he was still 'defined' as a 'tradesman' and expected, as he had been at Bury St Edmunds and Norwich, to play when required, coach members and provide practice facilities while acting as groundsman, a job previously occupied by a labourer. It comes as no surprise that Fuller apparently viewed the situation philosophically: 'Gentlemen were gentlemen, and players much in the same position as a nobleman and his head-keeper may be.'

---

8   About £5,000 a year in 2010 money.

*High Street, West Malling in the 1880s.
The George Inn, kept by Fuller Pilch from 1836 to 1842, is the two-storey building behind the man with the horse. The pub was rebuilt in the 1890s and then demolished to make way for a supermarket in 1971.*

Before playing for his new employers, Fuller had three engagements at Lord's, beginning with the 'Right-Handed v Left Handed' match on 13 and 14 July during which a new addition to the Laws was first applied: 'That the players who go in second shall follow their innings if they have obtained 100 runs less than their opponents.' Fuller was fortunate to have Redgate as a team-mate bowling down ten of the left-handers' wickets in the match after Fuller had initially compiled top score of 47 to help the right-handers to an innings victory. It was quite a different story a week later when the Players, including Fuller, met the Gentlemen who had their bowling line-up strengthened by the addition of Redgate and Cobbett. The Players registered their usual victory, but Redgate caused a sensation. *Scores and Biographies* reported it thus:- 'In this match the renowned Fuller Pilch was first opposed to Redgate in a double wicket match, and was bowled out by him for a nought in both innings!'

The following day a single-wicket match had been arranged at H.Hall's Ground in Camberwell with Mynn and Marsden teaming up to face Redgate and Good and there was great interest to see how Mynn would deal with the bowling of Redgate. But Redgate batted first and when missing a ball from Mynn he was struck such a blow on his knee that he was unable to bowl in the contest. As Fuller Pilch was present on the ground, hoping no doubt to have a chance to learn what he could from watching Mynn facing Redgate, he agreed to substitute as a fielder in the injured bowler's place.

Returning to Lord's the next week Fuller helped England beat Kent by innings with a top score of 59. The county fared no better in two matches against Town Malling, where Fuller settled in immediately with solid contributions with bat and ball. At Bromley on 3 and 4 August, thanks to Fuller's 22 out of 71, followed by an unbeaten 64, Town Malling won by five wickets, and in the return at Town Malling later in the month, on 25 August, Fuller's top score of 23 out of 138 helped the club to an innings victory. Thomas Selby and company must have realised that the sooner Fuller began playing for Kent the sooner they could begin to build a winning team around him. But the season was over and that must wait until next year while Fuller settled into his new employment and accommodation.

Chapter Twelve
Town Malling and Mr Pickwick

The year 1836 was the first that found Fuller fully resident in Kent and the beginning of a period when he played for an even greater number of teams than before. Apart from playing for his new employers, Town Malling, he appeared for Kent, England, MCC, The Players, Norfolk, The North, Nottingham, Benenden, and a Sussex club, Worth, at Crabbett Park.

He began by following his previous pattern of playing the early games of the summer close to home by playing five games in his new home county of Kent by the beginning of August, broken by four trips up to Lord's, including the first official North versus South match. From then onwards he went further afield to Leicester, Sheffield and Nottingham and a final appearance for Norfolk at Norwich, returning from time to time to Brighton and Kent. It would be another five years before Fuller went further north than St John's Wood, confining his activities to Kent, Surrey and Sussex.

But Fuller's journeys in 1836 would be overshadowed by an announcement in the press that an account of another person's 'perambulations, perils, travels, adventures and sporting transactions' would be published in monthly parts as 'The Posthumous Papers of the Pickwick Club'. Of particular interest to those that followed cricket was the appearance of Part Three in June, featuring the visit by Mr Pickwick and his companions to Manor Farm close to the Kent village of Dingley Dell and their attendance at a cricket match at the nearby town of Muggleton. From geographical clues it seems very likely that the author, Charles Dickens, had based his descriptions on a match he had witnessed at Town Malling before the arrival of Fuller Pilch, and an illustration in the book bears a great resemblance to views of the parish church from the cricket field. Indeed, Frederick Gale, writing of a 'grand match' at Town Malling, suggested that 'the description of which town, if put on paper, would so strongly resemble Muggleton in "Pickwick", that I have an idea that the real scene of the match between Muggleton and Dingley Dell may have been drawn from Town Malling.'

In common with most supporters wishing to attend any village match, Mr Pickwick and his friends set off in the afternoon on foot 'to the spot, where was to be held that trial of skill, which had roused all Muggleton from its torpor and inoculated Dingley Dell with a fever of excitement.' Their walk 'which was not above two miles long, lay through shady lanes and sequestered footpaths' and it was not long before they found themselves 'in the main street.' Describing the shops and services in the town, Dickens

Commemorative plaque at the Town Malling cricket ground in Norton Road. Kent played, in all, fourteen first-class matches here, including ten involving Fuller Pilch from 1836 to 1841.

West Malling village sign erected in 1986, depicting the village cricket match in Charles Dickens' Pickwick Papers. The bowler resembles Alfred Mynn and the batsman may be Felix.

draws particular attention to 'a red-brick house with a small paved court-yard in front, which anybody might have known belonged to the attorney' and this may have been his acknowledgement of the importance of the part played in the development of Town Malling as a famous cricket club by local solicitor Thomas Selby. Moving on to the cricket field Pickwick found 'The wickets were pitched, and so were a couple of marquees for the rest and refreshment of the contending parties.'

In his entertaining description of a typical game of cricket in the 1830s, Dickens certainly captured the spirit of good-humoured rivalry between two clubs of the time based only a mile or two apart, particularly when he moves on to dinner at the Blue Lion Inn where the victors All-Muggleton entertain the players of Dingley Dell and Mr Pickwick and his friends.

Back in the real world, Fuller began his season on 6 and 7 June at Lord's for MCC where his 15 out of 35 and 37 out of 110 could not stop Sussex winning by five wickets. This was the first match in the MCC scorebooks which had the addition of the bowler's names when a catch, stumping or lbw was made. It would take a few years but eventually this would become the practice at every club and bowling figures could be recorded in greater detail. Two weeks later, Fuller was engaged again by Benenden to play a two-day game against Kent at Hemsted Park, home of the West Kent MP, Twisden Hodges. It was one of those matches played on a private estate set up by wealthy benefactors that Fuller always enjoyed. Fred Gale reported him in *The Game of Cricket* as saying:

When they wanted a match they would send for Ned Wenman and me and say 'We want a good match; can you do it?' Well, then we used to reckon what it would come to, and they were at our backs if there was any money wanted; but we never asked for it if we made a good thing. Now don't you see here was the difference between those times and these; there were few railways, and matches were scarce, and some of our eleven put on different sides would draw all the country round for a two days' match in a nobleman's park; for instance, Mr Felix and Alfred Mynn were given one side, and Ned Wenman and me and Adams the other. Then, don't you see we were out for a two days' holiday, and the whole town enjoyed themselves, and the principal innkeepers used to arrange to have our company on different nights; and very often a lot of gentlemen would come too, and hear a song, for we had rare singing about in the county; and if Mr Felix had his fiddle with him – for he could make music on anything, from a church organ to a pair of tongs – it was a treat.

When Gale asked how he managed to play well the next day after a long evening at a local inn in such good company, Fuller explained: 'I used to manage that. Two glasses of gin-and-water were about my allowance; and when some of the company were asking me to drink, I told the landlord, "Let the gentlemen pay, and you leave the gin out of my glass"; and nobody knew it, but I was wetting my pipe with cold water half the evening.'

He certainly showed no ill-effects from any evening entertainment when scoring 107 for Benenden in their nine-wicket victory over Kent on 23 and 24 June, even though he was facing two great bowlers in Mynn and Hillyer. This was the first century scored against Kent since 1792. Benenden repeated their victory three days later at Leeds Park and even after Kent had joined forces with Sussex they were no match for England at Lord's on 4 July facing Fuller for the third consecutive time. In his next match, on 7, 8, and 9 July, he repaid the faith of his Town Malling sponsors with the top score of 37 out of 122 in their first innings at home to Kent, followed by an unbeaten 56 out of 153 in their second, although it was not enough to prevent a Kent four-wicket victory.

This was the year MCC decided that the time had come for a test of strength between the players of the North against those of the South. Two representative matches were arranged, the first at Lord's on 11 and 12 July and the second to be agreed later. The promoters were Lord Frederick Beauclerk and Benjamin Aislabie acting for MCC and the South, and our old friend Captain Cheslyn, now playing cricket in Leicestershire, for the North.

Although Fuller Pilch was no longer to be considered a 'given' man when playing for Town Malling in Kent, because of his residence there as club professional, it seems that, as he had not yet played for Kent, it was decided that Fuller should be in the North eleven because of his Norfolk qualification. It is unlikely that Fuller minded much as it meant he was on the same side as Redgate who took six wickets to help the North to their six-wicket victory.

The Gentlemen v Players match at Lord's followed on 25 and 26 July. This time MCC's attempts to balance the strengths of the two teams by allowing the Gentlemen to field eighteen players paid dividends as they won by 35 runs. Fuller went straight from Lord's to Gravesend to play on 28, 29 and 30 July for Town Malling against Kent, where, despite another half-century, 57 out of 140 in their second innings, it was not enough to prevent another win for Kent. Two days later he was at Chislehurst, again playing against Kent, but this time for the England Eleven on 1 and 2 August.

Fuller had not yet severed all his connections with Norfolk and he joined his brothers at Norwich for the annual match with Yorkshire. This brief return to the familiar fields of home in the first game on 4 and 5 August inspired him to prodigious efforts in a close-fought match. His 15 was top score in Norfolk's first innings of 52 in reply to Yorkshire's 114 and then he joined William to bowl them out in their second innings for 49, taking three wickets himself, with the other seven falling to his brother who finished with a match haul of twelve victims. This left Norfolk needing 112 to win and they crept closer and closer to victory but Fuller's undefeated 25 could not be supported and they finished 24 runs short.

Finally it was time for Fuller to represent his new county and it appears that Thomas Selby and company may have held back this historic event until it could be a feature of Kent's match on 8 and 9 August against Sussex on the ground at Town Malling, now known as 'Fuller Pilch's Ground'. The timing was perfect as more than 12,000 spectators were attracted to the match over the two days. To everyone's disappointment his debut innings was ended by Lillywhite before he had scored, and a desperate attempt in the second innings, top-scoring with 44 out of 131, failed to avert a loss by 32 runs.

The next week Fuller travelled with MCC to Brighton to face Sussex on 15, 16 and 17 August, but then it was time for a long journey up to Leicester for the second North v South challenge on 22, 23 and 24 August where, despite his new qualification for Kent, he was again selected to play for the North. The venue did not please the many enthusiasts in Nottingham, whose county had provided more than half of the North eleven, and hundreds of them walked the whole way between the two towns, determined to support their players. By 10 am on the first morning of the match, over 5,000 people were on the ground. The *Leicester Journal* reported 'so great an assemblage of Cricketers from all parts of the Kingdom were seldom or ever known to be collected together.' This was the famous match in which Alfred Mynn scored 125, despite batting for all of nearly five hours with an injured leg, and then being sent back to London immediately for medical treatment, travelling on the roof of a stage-coach because his leg had stiffened and he could not sit inside. The injury was so serious that one stage there were concerns he might have to lose the leg. Recovery was slow and he did not play cricket again for nearly two years.

His heroic efforts at Leicester were not in vain as the South won the match by 218 runs. Fuller Pilch was bowled by Lillywhite for nought in the first innings and out to the same bowler lbw for 28 in the second, but he was probably still happy not to have faced Redgate who took twelve wickets in the match.

Fuller remained in the north for the return Norfolk encounter with Yorkshire at Sheffield on 29, 30 and 31 August where the result was reversed as Norfolk squeezed home by one wicket, achieved with almost no contribution from Fuller. Going in at second wicket down he joined brother Nathaniel in Norfolk's first innings seeking to overtake Yorkshire's 60, everything was set for success until disaster struck. The *Sheffield Mercury* reported:

> Fuller Pilch – aye, Fuller, 'the pride of Norfolk' and 'terror of Sheffield', many not having forgot the 153 runs which he obtained in the last match at Sheffield, next made his appearance. The fielders altered their position and spread themselves wider in the field, evidently anticipating extra work from the skill of this well known batsman, but in this they were disappointed. Dearman had the first ball at this Prince of Cricketers, whom, as well as the second, he stopped, but the third lowered his wicket, to the astonishment of himself and every person on the ground – he retired without a run!

Norfolk still managed to secure a small first-innings lead and, after dismissing Yorkshire for 88, needed 79 to win. Everyone looked to Fuller to make amends for his first-innings failure and see Norfolk through to victory. The *Sheffield Mercury* reported:

> Fuller Pilch was then sent in to regain his lost laurels and received part of Mr Barker's over. The ball now passed to Dearman's end, and Hawkes got a run, which placed Fuller at the batting end. At this part of the game, a death-like silence prevailed amongst the spectators, which was followed by the most boisterous applause, Dearman having again lowered his wicket without a run. The Norfolk players were astonished, but not more than their opponents!

Putting these reversals behind him, four days later Fuller had accepted an engagement from Nottingham to play at the Forest Ground and made another century, 125 out of Nottingham's total of 197, that was less illustrious than others, 'taken as it was from the uneven bowling of his opponents', a twenty-two of the Nottingham New Forest and Bingham Club.'

Kent still had one more match to play, so Fuller hurried off down to Brighton to face Sussex on 12 and 13 September, but was unable to help prevent a win by seven wickets for the home county. After the game had finished at the end of two days instead of the scheduled three, it was decided to play a single innings match on 14 September. This was easily won by Sussex as well, after Kent were dismissed for 41 with Fuller bowled by Lillywhite, yet again, for nought. Sussex would not beat Kent again for another seven years. Four of the Kent players, including Fuller, played the next day for the Worth village team on F.S.Blunt's estate in Crabbett Park against an Uckfield team strengthened by five Brighton players. Then Fuller travelled back up to Nottingham for a repeat of the earlier match against the twenty-two of the New Forest and Bingham Club, spread over four days at the end of September. Nottingham won this match by nine wickets after Fuller's unbeaten 58 out of 137 in the first innings had given them a lead of 86.

Chapter Thirteen
Kent become the greatest team in England

Before Fuller Pilch started playing for Kent, they lost more than they won. After he joined the team in 1836 they won twice as many as they lost, until the decline that began in the early 1850s when age began to take its toll on the older players.

But the transformation did not happen overnight. Kent, with Fuller Pilch, had played Sussex twice in his first season and lost both games. There was a complete turnaround after that and in the five years from 1837 to 1841 Kent beat Sussex in eight consecutive matches. During the same period they played in all a total of 20 matches and won 15 of them, including five defeats of England elevens at Lord's and Town Malling. In those matches Fuller was the leading batsman for his new county, scoring 834 runs, including five half-centuries, with an average of 26.90. The next highest batsmen were Alfred Mynn with 343 runs, average 12.25, Ned Wenman with 304 runs, average 10.86, and Tom Adams 266 runs, average 8.09.

Nearly half of Kent's matches were played in front of huge crowds at Fuller Pilch's Ground at Town Malling, with the team selected by the Thomas Selby consortium, with advice from Fuller. There is a description by Frederick Gale of what it was like to attend one of those 'grand matches':

> It is five o'clock in the morning, and after a restless night, from anxiety and excitement, we are off in a trap of some kind for a twenty-miles drive to the match; and, as we leave Rochester and get into the Malling road, we find no dearth of company, and the road is much like a Derby-day at an early hour, as the old hands know very well that if they mean to get any stabling they must be early. Nor are the pedestrians less numerous than the riders. We pass many a poor fellow on the tramp, who has started over-night, perhaps, to be on the ground in time to see the first over, and to witness with his own eyes the feats of the mighty men of whom he has heard so much. And what a sight it is in town! All the inns are full of customers; and though it is only nine o'clock in the morning the horses are obliged to be stabled outside, with a canvas awning over them. And then, what a babel of voices we hear, interspersed with the north country dialect; as in an all-England match, the north countrymen who played, had their followers, just as the Kentish yeomen assembled to support their eleven. Let us go to the ground, for it is ten o'clock, and the match will begin at eleven to a moment, and we must get a seat in a hop-wagon early, or stand in the sun all day. Here come a lot of the players with a crowd of friends following them, in the hopes of seeing a little practice before the match

begins. Those two tall men are Alfred Mynn and Wenman, and the short man who has already begun to chaff Lillywhite is Mr Felix. Fuller Pilch and Joseph Guy of Nottingham, who are rivals for the honour of being the best batsmen in England, are walking side by side; and you can tell Pilch by his hands being crossed behind his back and a slight stoop in his gait.

Joseph Guy had made his debut for Nottinghamshire in 1837 and at Lord's the following year, playing for the North against the South, he was described in *Scores and Biographies* as 'a fine, upright, and scientific batsman, very forward in style, and could cut to the off and hit to the leg in a brilliant manner.' William Clarke said, famously, in *The Elevens of England* that he was 'all ease and elegance, fit to play before Her Majesty in a drawing-room.' The left-handed Nicholas Felix made his debut for Kent in 1834 and would soon establish himself as the most brilliant amateur batsman in England. Statistically though, neither Guy nor Felix could rival the success of Fuller Pilch.

During that five-year period 1837 to 1841, Fuller Pilch continued to play for a variety of teams and clubs as well as Town Malling and Kent, and was the leading batsman in England for four of those five seasons, overtaken only once by Felix in 1840. According to the statistics compiled by Keith Warsop for his article in *The Cricket Quarterly* mentioned earlier, the figures were in 1837, 544 runs, average 32.00; in 1838, 486 runs, average 22.09; in 1839, 624 runs, average 25.14; in 1840, 500 runs, average 19.23 (second to Felix who scored 203 runs, average 22.55); and in 1841, 618 runs, average 24.72. My own more recent research shows that Fuller scored 521 runs in 1840 with a lower average of 17.37.

> And whatever was the issue of the frank and friendly fray,
> (Aye, and often has his bowling turned the issue of the day),
> Still the Kentish men fought bravely, never losing hope or heart,
> Every man of the eleven glad and proud to play his part.
> And with five such mighty cricketers, 'twas but natural to win,
> As Felix, Wenman, Hillyer, Fuller Pilch, and Alfred Mynn.

An early printing of the verse by W.J.Prowse recording Kent's primacy. The press recorded Kent as 'champion county' in six of the seven seasons from 1837 to 1843.

The 1837 season started well for Fuller on 12 and 13 June at Town Malling with 44 out of 103 in Kent's first innings and, although he was bowled by Lillywhite for nought in the second, Kent beat Sussex by two wickets. Huge numbers of spectators were on the ground, at least 10,000 each day, and many wagers were made as the game progressed. Not everyone in West Malling welcomed the invasion by so many outsiders and the following Sunday the vicar preached against the game of cricket that brought the evils of gambling into his parish.

A week later Sussex went up to Lord's to play an MCC side strengthened by Fuller, Wenman and Redgate and proved that they were still a force to be reckoned with, winning by three wickets. Fuller top-scored in the first MCC innings with 30 out of 82 and might have done even better in the second if he had not been run out on 13. Kent went down to Brighton to face Sussex in the last week of June and won by three wickets, thanks to Fuller's unbeaten 69 in the second innings chasing 152. Then came the traditional Gentlemen v Players fixture on 3 and 4 July where MCC repeated the idea of making the Players defend a larger wicket, this time with four stumps 36 inches by 12 inches while the Gentlemen defended three stumps according to the latest Laws, 27 inches by 8 inches. It was called the 'Barn-Door Match' and the difference in the size of wickets had no effect as the Players won by an innings in a low-scoring match where Fuller was out for nine when dismissed by Sir Frederick Hervey-Bathurst, fast bowler and baronet, 'hat knocked on wicket'.

But the most important match that summer was the North against the South challenge in mid-July at Lord's to celebrate the fiftieth anniversary of MCC. The game had been announced the year before by Benjamin Aislabie, the MCC secretary, and noted in the club minutes, as follows:

> The Marylebone Club having been established in the year 1787, it is resolved that a Jubilee Match shall take place at Lord's Ground on the second Monday in July 1837, for the benefit of the players; twenty-two of whom shall be chosen to perform on that day. The Earl of Thanet and the Lord Frederick Beauclerk are requested to make the selection: and every Member of the Club is solicited for a subscription of One Pound towards the promotion of the sport on this interesting occasion.

This time Fuller was chosen to play for the South and made 13 out of their first innings total of 60 before being dismissed by Redgate. He was held back in the second innings but the South reached the 70 runs target after losing only five wickets. Three thousand spectators attended on both days, including a 'long list of fashionables'. After the match, all the players were guests at a Jubilee dinner 'served up in Mr Dark's usual excellent style and consisted of every delicacy of the season' according to *Bell's Life*.

Eleven players from the Jubilee match, five from the North and six from the South, returned to Lord's a week later to face 'Sixteen Gentlemen'. Haygarth said some of these had been selected only because they 'happened to be on the ground.' It was no surprise that the Players, with a score of 154 including 34 from Fuller, won by an innings and 38 runs with Lillywhite taking eighteen wickets.

Nottinghamshire had arrived in the south of England to play Sussex at Brighton on 24, 25 and 26 July, and then on the following two days met Kent for the first time, losing at Town Malling by nine wickets. Fuller was lbw for five runs in his only innings, the bowler unidentified but possibly Redgate. Two weeks later Fuller was in Surrey to record the highest score of his career, 160 for Town Malling against Reigate. *Scores and Biographies* tells us: 'Fuller Pilch's enormous innings – which is, perhaps the most wonderful on record, because obtained against William Lillywhite's bowling – exceeded the whole of the twenty-two innings of the Reigate party.'

Fuller joined Redgate and Wenman at Brighton to play against Sussex on 14 and 15 August and helped MCC to a six-wicket victory. In the return match between Town Malling and Reigate on 17 and 18 August Fuller could only manage three and nine, although none of the two clubs four innings totalled more than 47. Then Fuller went up to Chislehurst to play as a given man for the Gentlemen of Kent against MCC where his twelve runs as recorded in the scorebook attracted the attention of *Scores and Biographies*: 'Pilch's runs were made by a five, a six and a one.'

The start of Fuller's closer association with Sussex began with his last appearance of the season on 18, 19 and 20 September as a given man for Sussex against England at Brighton where top scores of 38 and 84 helped them to a victory by 79 runs. Kent supporters were not alarmed by what they assumed was a one-off engagement. Further engagements in 1838 and 1839 would, though, create more concern when they feared they might be about to lose their 'Champion'.

Kent become the greatest team in England

G.F.Watts' well-known lithograph of 1837, featuring Fuller Pilch in braces and trade-mark top hat, with an unspliced bat. The headgear fell on his wicket at Lord's on 3 July 1837, an incident referred to in a Duckworth Lewis Method recording made in 2009, in which 'topper' rhymed with 'cropper'.

Chapter Fourteen
A new Champion of England

The most famous cricket event of 1838 did not actually feature Fuller, although he was very much involved. Three years earlier a letter had appeared in *Bell's Life* signed by Alfred Mynn:

> Sir,
>
> Having been much annoyed by numerous letters and inquiries in consequence of a reported match of single wicket, for 100 guineas, between Mr Fuller Pilch and myself, you will perhaps oblige me by inserting this letter, as the only means of checking any further annoyance to me. I am open to Mr Fuller Pilch, or any other player in England, from £20 to £50 a side, for a single wicket match at cricket, between this and the 31st of August, provided it is played at Lord's or the Camberwell Ground. If, however, Mr Pilch feels inclined to accept the challenge, time, place, and amount of stake, may be easily arranged, by applying to Mr Hall at his Cricket-ground, Camberwell.
>
> I am, Sir, obediently yours,
>
> A.Mynn

The letter seems to confirm a straightforward challenge, but all was not as it seemed. A few weeks later an announcement appeared in the columns of *Bell's Life*:

> We have authority for saying that the challenge in our paper of the 21st ult from Alfred Mynn to Fuller Pilch, was without the consent of the former. The fact is, that within the last three months there was a private offer, on the part of a friend of Mynn's, to back him against Fuller Pilch granting the latter the privilege of naming his own sum, time, and place, but the friends of Pilch declined the invitation.'

It seems that someone had seen the financial potential of a meeting between Fuller Pilch and Mynn and had tried to create a situation where neither player would be able to withdraw without suffering damage to their reputations. But, despite his easy single-wicket victory over Thomas Marsden two years earlier, Fuller had no interest in defending his title, and certainly not if it meant facing his friend and soon-to-be Kent team-mate Alfred Mynn. Three years later he seems to have changed his mind after an announcement appeared in *Bell's Life* on 13 May 1838 saying that James Dearman of Yorkshire would be backed against any man in England at single wicket for £100, which received an anonymous reply on May 27, revealed later by Thomas Selby as coming from Fuller Pilch, who was now apparently happy to face anyone other than Alfred Mynn:

> Sir,
>
> In answer to Mr Dearman's challenge in your paper today to play at single wicket with any man in England. I beg leave to accept that challenge, and hereby offer to make the match: to play home and away for £100 each match, and to toss for the choice of the place of playing the third or conquering match for a similar sum should each party win one of the two matches. I wish to avoid advertising my name, and will therefore merely add that I live within 35 miles of London, and am Sir, yours respectfully,
>
> A Cricketer

There was a note added by *Bell's Life:* 'Should Dearman agree to the above, we will furnish him with the means of ascertaining who the Cricketer is, and where the match can be made.'

Soon after it was reported that Mr G.Hardesty of Sheffield, acting rather like a modern-day boxing promoter, was ready to make the match on Dearman's behalf in a contest with Fuller Pilch. A month later Fuller withdrew and chose to name Alfred Mynn in his place. The first match was at Town Malling on 20 August with Fuller supervising all the arrangements, which contradicts the suggestion that the challenge had been taken up by Mynn because of Fuller's numerous engagements, rather than because he preferred to opt out of something that he did not enjoy if expected to be one of the two players, whatever the prize money on offer.

The Dearman party arrived the day before play was due to start and were met at Rochester by Mynn in a carriage lent by Thomas Selby, who also offered them all hospitality at his home. Mynn took the affair very seriously, as he was always struggling financially and could do with the money, and had actually gone into training to improve his fitness. Patrick Morrah in *Alfred Mynn and the Cricketers of his Time*, published in 1986, says that while preparing to meet his opponent he asked Pilch: 'Fuller, do I look fit to play today?' There was no doubt in his friend's mind: 'Why, he looked fit to carry a church and a whole congregation round the town.'

There were 5,000 spectators on the ground to see Mynn win easily by 112 runs, followed afterwards by an impromptu three-a-side single-wicket game to give the crowd some further entertainment, which featured Hardesty, Mynn and Dearman against Pilch, Redgate and 'a gentleman on the ground'. There was a similar large crowd at Sheffield a week later to witness Mynn's victory by 36 runs in the return match and so the title 'Champion of England' changed hands.

Chapter Fifteen
Attracted by the seaside charms of Sussex

Fuller Pilch played as many matches in Sussex in 1838 as he did in Kent and twice as often in 1839. Eventually Kent would have to make him an offer that he could not refuse.

His 1838 season started in June with two games for Town Malling against a side representing the Kent village of Leeds. The two clubs contained most of the best players in Kent and this proved good preparation for the season to come. The first, on 5 and 6 June at Town Malling, was won by Leeds, thanks to Mynn bowling down ten wickets in the match. In the second, at Leeds a few days later, Town Malling had their revenge by 23 runs, with Fuller making top score of 18 out of 79 in their second innings. Then Fuller went to Lord's to play for MCC against Sussex on 18 and 19 June and a week later was back at Lord's to play in another special North *v* South match arranged to take advantage of the crowds that had swarmed into London for the Coronation of Queen Victoria on 28 June. Fuller rose to the occasion and made top score of the match with 64 in the first innings for the South, when not even the combined attack of Lillywhite and Redgate could dislodge him and only some swift action in the field to run him out prevented him from reaching an even higher score.

After the Coronation match, Fuller joined Kent for two consecutive matches with Sussex in July. Kent won by 76 runs at Brighton on 12, 13 and 14 July and narrowly by two wickets at Town Malling a week later. The result of the second game might have been different if the coach bringing the Sussex team had not been upset and some of the visiting players suffered minor injuries. Even so, it needed a masterly 42 from Fuller to get Kent's first innings up to 93 and a winning lead of 29. For the Gentlemen *v* Players match at Lord's at the end of July, Fuller joined Cobbett and Wenman to strengthen the Gentlemen who were without Mynn. This meant that Fuller had to face a rampant Redgate who took nine wickets in the match to help the Players win by 40 runs. Fuller was dismissed twice by his nemesis but not before he had made top score of 21 in the Gentlemen's second innings.

Kent only played one other match that year when they lost by ten wickets to Benenden at Hemsted Park on 6 and 7 August, after Fuller was bowled by Mynn in both innings. Then Fuller was off to Brighton where he made 42 in the MCC first innings of 114 but was not needed in the second innings of their six-wicket victory over Sussex on 13 and 14 August. He stayed on in Brighton and at the end of the month he was engaged as a given man for Sussex against a strong England team in which all the players were Kent and Nottinghamshire men, including Redgate, who only captured three wickets in the match, none of them Fuller's, while Sussex won easily by 85 runs. Then it was time for Fuller to return to Town Malling to play Benenden on 10 and 11 September and score 58 out of the home side's only innings of 122 in an unfinished match. But he could not resist the opportunity to go back to Brighton for the last two weeks of September where he was engaged to play twice for the Gentlemen of Sussex against the Players of Sussex. The Gentlemen won the first encounter by three wickets but lost the second by 102 runs, despite Fuller's 67 out of 161 in their first innings followed by the top score of 23 out of 70 in the second.

By now many supporters of Kent must have realised that there was a real danger of losing their star batsman to their neighbours. Positive action would be needed next season and all eyes turned to Thomas Selby at West Malling. But if the powers behind cricket in Kent had been worried about the temptations put before Fuller by Sussex in 1838, the first six weeks of 1839 would give them even greater cause for alarm.

In the absence of any offers from clubs in Kent, Fuller played five games in Sussex between 27 May and 5 July, interrupted only by a visit to Lord's to play for MCC against Sussex and joining Kent for their first game of the season at Brighton.

Fuller began at Brighton on 27, 28 and 29 May, playing for the Sussex village of Chalvington against a strong eleven from the Brighton Club that included a number of Sussex county regulars, among them William Lillywhite. Keen to impress, Fuller even took a turn at bowling and captured some wickets, but he surpassed himself with the bat when Chalvington had to follow on 119 runs behind, and he recorded another century, 114 out of 208, that almost won the game before Brighton squeezed home by two wickets. *Scores and Biographies* said of this: 'Pilch's batting in this match, considering the bowling he had to contend against, was something marvellous.' Then it was time to travel up to London where he was engaged by MCC to play against Sussex at Lord's on 10 and 11 June. After making only one in the first innings, he was at the wicket with an unbeaten 16 in the second when MCC completed their win by seven wickets.

For the next 24 days Fuller concentrated his activities exclusively within the county of Sussex. Another appearance for Chalvington came first on 19 and 20 June, with 38 out of 59 in their first innings in reply to 140, followed by nought when bowled by Lillywhite in a second Chalvington innings that only reached 21 when losing to Brighton by 106 runs. Then it was back in to Brighton where he was engaged to play for the Gentlemen of Sussex against the Players of Sussex. He stayed by the sea until the beginning of July to await the arrival of the Kent team to come down for their first match of the season to face Sussex. The hosts failed to capitalise on a first innings lead of 47 runs and Kent reached their target of 110 to win with only two wickets in hand thanks to an unbeaten 38 from Fuller. The Kent team returned home without Fuller and the next day he was in Chalvington to help the village finally record a victory over Brighton who, this time, were without Lillywhite. It would be nearly six weeks before he would savour the sea air of Sussex again as the powers of Kent cricket laid their plans to keep him where they believed he belonged, while he played three matches in their county and three at Lord's.

On 8 and 9 July, Fuller helped MCC beat England at Lord's by six wickets and then joined Penshurst at Benenden where his 48 out of 105 in the second innings saved them from defeat with the game unfinished. It was back to Lord's for England's innings and a one-run victory over a combined Nottinghamshire and Sussex eleven on 23 and 24 July and then five days later contributing 28 to the Players massive first innings of 235 runs from 574 balls against a Gentlemen eleven playing without any given men who would have lost by an innings if rain had not intervened.

Kent's return match against Sussex, at Town Malling on 5 and 6 August, was another triumph for Fuller with top score of 41 out of 112 in the first innings and 37 out of 77 in the second that saw another Kent victory by three wickets. Three days later he was at Penshurst where his unbeaten 48 out of 94 gave them a first innings lead of 26 over Benenden, but a second innings collapse saw Benenden earn victory by four wickets.

Still keeping his options open, Fuller then accepted another engagement to play for the Gentlemen of Sussex at Brighton on 15 and 16 August, this time against MCC. His top score of 36 out of 128 in the second innings was another demonstration that, whichever county secured his services, they would certainly be receiving value for their money.

Fred Gale reported in *Echoes From Old Cricket Fields*, published in 1871, that when the fixture lists were being prepared for the 1839 season it had been generally recognised that Kent 'was the only county which could contend against England' and a match was duly arranged between them, the first for three years. Kent supporters hoped this would demonstrate to Fuller that Kent was the place to be. MCC had agreed to send the strongest England team they could find to Town Malling for the match on 19, 20 and 21 August and now Thomas Selby announced that he had persuaded the powers at Lord's to take over as patrons, with Lord Frederick Beauclerk as manager of the England team. But the biggest news of all was that the match would be played as a benefit for Fuller Pilch, now in his thirty-sixth year.

The usual large crowds gathered, with the ground roped and enclosed by wagons. Kent won the toss and made 145, thanks to 35 from Fuller and 37 from Wenman, facing the bowling of Lillywhite, Cobbett and Redgate: 'Whether the balls came fast or slow, creeping grounders or regular flings, Pilch and Wenman knew exactly how to take them and frequently elicited the admiration of the company by the style in which they played,' reported the *Maidstone Journal*. When Kent batted again they were 15 runs in front and had reached 30 without loss when lightning struck. Redgate was brought into the attack and in his first over completely changed the game in England's favour. His first ball bowled opener Stearman and Redgate celebrated with a glass of brandy brought out to him while waiting for Alfred Mynn to take his place at the wicket. One ball later he was drinking another brandy as Mynn returned to the marquees and a potential England victory prompted a flood of wagers from their supporters. Fuller was next and he survived the third ball of the over before the fourth shattered his wicket and the bowler had another brandy in his hand while even larger sums were being wagered on an England victory. Then Lillywhite got to work and claimed five victims while Redgate, showing no ill-effects from his earlier celebrations, bowled another 56 balls to take two more wickets. England only needed 80 to win and when last man Lillywhite was at the wicket they were only three runs short. A gentleman offered Hillyer five pounds if he could dismiss Lillywhite in the next over and the first ball just missed the wicket. The next ball shattered the stumps and Kent were winners by two runs.

After the match Fuller revealed that he had indeed received a generous offer that was too good to ignore from Sussex who had now formally established themselves as a County Cricket Club. Kent sponsors put their heads together and then convinced him that there were plans in progress to develop cricket in Kent even further, also including formation as a County Cricket Club, and that he stood to gain financially if he stayed where he was considered the county's prime asset. An official announcement followed. The Kent history by Lord Harris and F.S Ashley-Cooper, published in 1929, reported it thus:

> Pilch mentioned at the termination of this match that he had received such an encouraging proposition from the county of Sussex that he should not feel justified in rejecting it. The gentlemen present, however, determined that, whatever proposition Sussex might make, Kent would exceed it. It gives us great pleasure to announce that, Mr Pilch has determined to remain in Kent. Our cricketing friends will rejoice at this, for we believe that a more respectable, well-balanced, and generally respected man never came into the county.

In later years Fuller would reveal to Gale that leaving Kent was never really an option:

> ... bless my soul! As soon as any man had been twelve months amongst the cherry orchards and hop-gardens and the pretty Kent girls, he couldn't help becoming Kent to the backbone. Why, look at the support we had, and look at the money in the county. All the land almost was held by rich noblemen and gentlemen; and the farmers many of them were worth their twenty thousand pounds, and farmed very high, and had leisure to enjoy themselves. Why the cherries would go on a-growing, and the hop-bine keep on creeping, night and day, whilst they were looking at a cricket match. Think of our supporters – Mr Wykeham Martyn, Mr Twisden Hodges, Lord Sondes, Lord Harris, Mr Selby of Town Malling, and half a score more in the county.

Attracted by the seaside charms of Sussex

Despite his decision to stay committed to Kent it appears that when the county or Town Malling did not need him, Fuller had reserved the right to play where he wished. As he had previously agreed to play for Chalvington at Brighton immediately after the match at Town Malling, that would be his next appearance and he helped the village to achieve another victory.

An injury, unidentifiable at this distance in time, forced Fuller to miss the last two matches for Town Malling against Mitcham in September, but his friend Alfred Mynn was ready and willing to act as his replacement and Fuller had recovered sufficiently to be able to umpire in the second game at Town Malling. But he was not fit enough to travel and Alfred helped him out again three days later at Brighton against an England eleven. *Scores and Biographies* reported that 'F.Pilch was to have been the given man for Sussex, but was unable to come owing to injury, and Mr A.Mynn played instead.'

This is perhaps the right point in the story to review Fuller's position as a batsman in the ten seasons 1830 to 1839. Though first-class cricket is only part of his cricketing tale, that particular form of the game provides us with the most orderly array of statistics. He had been the leading run-scorer in six of those ten seasons, 1830, 1832, 1834, and 1837 to 1839. In the ten seasons he had scored 2,564 runs at an average of 23.96. Wickets in first-class matches in those ten seasons were worth on average 9.92 runs apiece, so he scored runs at 2.41 times the average cost. In modern times we have become accustomed in England to wickets in first-class cricket having a value of around 34 runs each; Fuller's batting achievements were thus the modern-day equivalent of a batting average, over the ten seasons, of a few decimal points short of 82!

Chapter Sixteen
The growing influence of the Beverley Club

By now there were indications that Town Malling was being overtaken as the most important club in the county as the increasing influence of country-house sponsored clubs was changing the face of Kent cricket.

In 1835 the Beverley Club had been formed by the Reverend John Baker and his brother William de Chair Baker, to play on St. Stephen's Field, part of the family estate behind their house 'Beverley', near Hackington, a small village on the outskirts of Canterbury. The club's matches became great social occasions and the hospitality of the Bakers was famous throughout Kent. Country-house cricket was growing in popularity with the owners of estates all over the county. It was a good way to entertain friends, neighbours, tenants and nearby villagers. Amateur cricketers would come for the good food and fine wine, some of them eligible young bachelors and suitable company for unmarried daughters. To raise the standard of the cricket to be played over two or three days, famous professionals were paid top rates and housed at local inns.

Over the next few years the Beverley Club established itself as a team of some importance, and was often referred to as the 'Canterbury Club' while enjoying regular fixtures with the teams from Adisham, Aikham, Aluph, Ash, Boughton, Dover, Faversham, Ickham, Leeds, Minster, Preston, Sandwich and Sittingbourne. But the annual matches with Chilston, a team sponsored by James Stoddard Douglas at his estate in Chilston Park, became the highlights of the season. To many, Beverley represented East Kent and Chilston West Kent, and the *Kentish Gazette* reported matches attracting 'between three and four thousand spectators ... many of them elegantly dressed ladies'.

In 1839 Douglas had hired Alfred Mynn to play for Chilston in both games against Beverley, who themselves engaged the services of two top-class players, William Clifford and Nicholas Felix. Thousands turned out to watch the first game at Beverley; the *Gazette* reported that 'several booths were erected, and the whole neighbourhood leading from the city presented the appearance of a fair.' The rivalry intensified in 1840, with both clubs seeking to strengthen their teams even further and their 'Grand Cricket Match', at Chilston Park on 16 and 17 July, was advertised as being between 'eight gentlemen of the Chilston Club, with three players, and nine gentlemen of Beverley, with two players.' Not surprisingly, Fuller Pilch, described as 'the best batsman that has ever yet appeared', was one of the professionals engaged by Chilston who again featured Alfred Mynn, plus Stearman and Wenman. They were not strong enough to defeat a Beverley side that already had Felix and Clifford before adding Hillyer, Charles Taylor and Alfred Mynn's brother Walter. The return fixture took place a week later on a field next to the Cavalry Barracks, outside the North Gate in the Canterbury city walls. This ground was hired by Beverley from a local farmer, John Sneller, as part of the club's bold and ambitious plans to strengthen relationships with the city. More well-known cricketers were added to the teams, Lillywhite for Chilston, Redgate and Hawkins for Beverley, and the match attracted enormous interest, according to the *Kentish Gazette*, with crowds of between 1,500 and 2,000 on both days occupying 'marquees, tents, benches and accommodation of all kinds' despite Beverley charging an entrance fee for the first time. Refreshments 'served up in first-rate style' were available and the band of the 13th Dragoons, quartered in the Barracks next door, played on the ground every day. Fuller rose to the occasion with an undefeated top score of 59 in Chilston's first innings; he top-scored again with 49 in the second, to give the visitors a repeat victory.

News of the success of the occasion even found its way to the desk of Lord Hill, Commander-in-Chief of the Army, who issued orders that cricket grounds should be built at every Army barracks throughout Britain, in the belief that spare time spent playing cricket, a game which embodied the 'virtues of strength, persistence, courage, leadership and sportsmanship', and would provide a moral and character-building distraction from the more usual off-duty pursuits of soldiers – drink and prostitutes.

Fuller's own 1840 season had started earlier, on 28 May, with two matches in Sussex, playing for Goodwood against West Sussex and three days later at Lewes for Alfriston against The Priory. The Sussex connection continued when he appeared as a given man for the county against England at Lord's on 8 and 9 June. Then he was back at Town Malling on 18, 19 and 20 June for the county match between Kent and Nottinghamshire. He was bowled by Redgate for only three in the first innings and Kent needed 116 runs to avoid an innings defeat when they batted again. Fuller's 63 out of 120, falling to a catch off Clarke, meant Nottinghamshire only had to bat briefly again to register an impressive victory by ten wickets.

Two days later Fuller faced Redgate again in the Slow Bowlers *v* Fast Bowlers encounter at Lord's and the Nottingham bowler dismissed him in both innings for nought and eight. They were together at Lord's on 29 and 30 June to help the Players beat the Gentlemen by nine wickets, but on July 6 were back on opposite sides when England faced Kent. Fuller was dismissed cheaply in both innings but not by Redgate as it was Lillywhite who did all the damage taking 15 wickets in the match to help England win by 76 runs

The Beverley and Chilston matches in July had been part of a sequence of six consecutive appearances in Kent made by Fuller over a three-week period that year, including two games for Town Malling against Penshurst, another at Tunbridge Wells where he and Lillywhite were given men for Hastings and St Leonards against the local club strengthened by Mynn and

Wenman, and then joining Wenman as a pair of given men for the Updown Club on John Bayley's ground near Sandwich against MCC.

During these matches Fuller recorded his greatest performance as a bowler. Playing for Town Malling on 27 July, in the second match against Penshurst, he took all ten first-innings wickets, demonstrating that, while round-arm bowling continued to dominate, there was still a place for under-arm bowling if the bowler was expert in its application.

After the group of games in Kent, Fuller joined Sussex again at Brighton on 10 and 11 August to face the England eleven including Redgate who failed to take his wicket. Fuller's 24 out of 65 in the Sussex second innings was not enough to prevent England winning by four wickets. A week later he played at Town Malling for Kent facing most of the same England team strengthened by three Sussex players, including Lillywhite, who took eight wickets, but failed like Redgate to dismiss Fuller in either innings. Fuller's 46 out of Kent's 110 gave them enough of a first-innings lead to ensure Kent's victory by three wickets. There was just time to fit in an engagement for Penshurst against Benenden at Penshurst Park on 27 and 28 August before Fuller rejoined Kent at Bromley to meet England for their third encounter on 3, 4 and 5 September. It was a very weak Kent eleven, lacking five regular players, and nobody reached double figures in either innings, in both of which Fuller top-scored with eight and nine, falling to Redgate in the first innings and Lillywhite in the second. This was Fuller's last match in 1840 when, as luck would have it, his 19-year-old nephew William was present. Ned Wenman was hit in the mouth while keeping wicket during England's first innings and had to withdraw. William stepped up to take the injured player's place in the field and as Kent had not yet batted he was allowed to bat as well. A somewhat unusual county debut and it would be another four years before young Pilch played for Kent again.

Fuller's first county match of 1841 was at Brighton on 7 and 8 June to face Sussex and his top score of 53 played a major role in Kent's innings victory. The Sunday before the game started was the day of the 1841 Census, 6 June, and eight Kent players, Fuller Pilch, Alfred Mynn, Walter Mynn, Ned Wenman, Dorrinton, Martingell, Clifford and Mills, had stayed overnight at the Bear Inn in Lewes. The opportunity to learn the address of Fuller's residence in Town Malling at that time was thus lost. It is interesting to note, however, that he preferred to enter his occupation as 'tailor' and not 'cricketer' and, by so doing, even ignored his position as 'innkeeper' back at Town Malling. At least it does confirm that he had continued to practice his original profession (and that he needed to) despite the demands on his time travelling the roads of England playing cricket for a living and managing an inn on his return.

Fuller returned to Town Malling from Sussex before heading off ten days later to Gravesend with the club to lose badly to the home side by 141 runs. Three days later he played in the 'Fast Bowlers *v* Slow Bowlers' match at Lord's on June 21, 22 and 23 June which had established itself as a popular fixture. This time he was selected to strengthen the Fast Bowlers eleven and avoided the fast bowling of Redgate. He was dismissed by Lillywhite in both innings, but top-scored with 39 out of 90 in the second innings while sharing a long partnership with Redgate in a failed attempt to avoid defeat.

Fuller was back at Lord's on 29 and 30 June as a given man for the Gentlemen of England, joining both Mynn brothers to play in a never-to-be-repeated match against an Old Etonian eleven assisted by Lillywhite, Cobbett and Hillyer. This fixture ended as a surprising win for the Old Etonians despite efforts from Fuller, who scored 57 of the total of 135 runs compiled by the Gentlemen in their two innings and Mynn, who took 11 Etonian wickets. MCC decided to stage another Fast Bowlers v Slow Bowlers match the following week with Fuller once more in the Fast Bowlers side which reversed the earlier result. After that, Fuller appeared on the opposite side to Beverley, playing for Dover in a match in early July which featured, according to its publicity, 'twelve of the most celebrated players in England', including Lillywhite, Wenman and Hillyer for Beverley and Mynn, Box, Clifford, Cobbett and Pilch for Dover. The home side won by five wickets thanks to an unbeaten 41 from Fuller in the second innings.

Fuller had left Dover to go up to Lord's to play in the Gentlemen v Players annual fixture on 12 and 13 July, won by the Players as usual, but narrowly by three wickets, thanks to Fuller's top score of 32 in the second innings. He returned to Canterbury to help Beverley beat Dover by six wickets in the return match on July 15, 16 and 17 July, where the *Kentish Gazette* noted 'A large party of fashionables honoured the field with their company [and the] playing was considered exceedingly good, and gave the highest satisfaction to the numerous spectators.'

Then it was time for Fuller to rejoin the Kent ranks for a six-wicket victory over Sussex at Town Malling on 22, 23 and 24 July, followed by successive wins over England at Lord's by 70 runs on 26 and 27 July and at Town Malling by two wickets at the end of the month. These successes inspired the Kent promoters to approach the Beverley Club with a request to stage a third match on their new ground at Canterbury on 10, 11 and 12 August thereby spreading interest in county cricket from West into East Kent. It was a huge success on all three days of the match, as the *Kentish Gazette* commented: 'About 4,000 persons assembled on the beautiful ground of the Beverley Cricketers, which was in as fine order as attention could make it.' Fuller top-scored for Kent in their first innings with 43 out of 114 and Mynn took 11 wickets but, to the surprise of everyone, England won by 74 runs, with Kent collapsing to 31 all out in their second innings. Redgate took seven wickets in the match but failed to dismiss Fuller who fell to Lillywhite in both innings.

Some Kent supporters had lost money in wagers on this outcome and rumours of a 'fix' began to circulate. The accusation was strenuously denied in the *Kent Herald* some months later:

> To any knowing the parties thus accused, and possessing either principle or honour, this rumour will seem preposterous, but as there

CRICKET.

A GRAND MATCH
WILL BE PLAYED IN
LORD'S GROUND,
MARYLEBONE,
On MONDAY, JUNE 21st, 1841,
And following Day.

The Slow Bowlers of England against the Fast

PLAYERS.

Slow Bowlers.	Fast Bowlers.
BAYLEY,	A. MYNN, Esq.
COBBETT,	C. G. WHITTAKER, Esq.
LILLYWHITE,	REDGATE,
The Hon. Capt. LIDDELL.	N. BLAND, Esq.
E. BARNETT, Esq.	R. W. KEATE, Esq.
R. KYNASTON, Esq.	C. W. A. NAPIER, Esq.
C. G TAYLOR, Esq.	W. PICKERING, Esq.
F. THACKERAY, Esq.	Captain PRICE,
J. M. WYTHE, Esq.	W. WARD, Esq.
GUY,	BOX,
WENMAN.	PILCH,

MATCHES TO COME.

Monday, June 28, at Lord's, Nine Gentlemen old Etonians, with Lillywhite & Hillyer, against Eleven Gentlemen of England.
Thursday, July 1st, at Lord's, the Marylebone Club, against the Undergraduates of Cambridge
Monday, July 5th, at Lord's, the Marylebone Club & Ground, against the Nottingham Club and Ground.

Cricket Bats, Balls, Stumps, Score Papers and the Laws of Cricket as revised by the Marylebone Club in 1838, to be had of Mr. J. H. DARK, at the Pavilion, and at the Manufactory on the Ground.

AN ORDINARY AT THREE O'CLOCK.
Admittance 6d.   Good Stabling on the Ground.   No Dogs Admitted.

MORGAN, Printer, 39, New Church Street, Portman Market.

Handbill for a famous MCC match in 1841.
Fuller is on the same side as his bête-noire, Samuel Redgate. Fuller himself was rarely, if ever, a fast bowler.

may be some prone to censure without giving themselves time to reflect, it may be well to say a few words. Who is the man that would be bold enough to attempt to purchase the honour of eleven Kentish cricketers, numbering (without being invidious to others) the names of Baker, Mynn, Pilch, Wenman, and Dorrington? Such a man would no more dare to show his face on a cricket field again than the men who could be so basely bought. This villainous report emanated from some sordid 'snob', who had missed winning his sixpence by the match, and thus vomited forth his frothy poison, and what at first was an idle tale became a serious speculation. If such a thing were possible, would it be done so barefacedly? Would five good men have gone out without a run when a hundred runs were wanting? Perish such a thought with him who dares to think it. Did anyone hear that England's eleven was sold when the men of Kent put them out at Lord's on the 26th and 27th of July last year for 31 and 44 runs? Surely no more need be said.

Fuller continued his 1841 season by umpiring a couple of Town Malling matches against Yalding on August 16 and 23 before joining the Kent team on a visit to Nottingham to play Nottinghamshire at Trent Bridge on August 26, 27 and 28. Redgate was unable to play for the home side and Fuller's top score of 48 out of 130 set Kent up for a win by 22 runs despite J.N.Dudlow going missing and batting with only ten men. Two days later six of the Kent team, including Fuller, were appearing as given men for Tunbridge Wells at home to Sevenoaks who themselves had engaged seven given men including Redgate. Fuller top-scored with 43 out of 149 in the home side's first innings and Sevenoaks eventually gave up the match before even attempting to reach the 226 runs they needed to win. The Kent team re-assembled at the White Hart Ground behind the White Hart Inn in Bromley on 13 and 14 September to beat a weak England team by an innings and ten runs. Redgate bowled only 24 balls in England's innings and again failed to dismiss Fuller, who top-scored with 20 out of 104 to end his year on a high note.

STATE OF THE MATCH OF CRICKET

PLAYED AT WEST MALLING, KENT.
The 29th and 30th of July, 1841
Between

KENT & ENGLAND.

ENGLAND	1st Innings	2nd Inn.
Box c A Mynn	5—	c Whittaker 3
Sampson c A Mynn	14—	b Hillyer 1
Hawkins c W Mynn	0—	c Mills 7
Ward esq c Pilch	1—	c Mills 3
Redgate run out	8—	b Hillyer 3
Sewell b Hillyer	13—	c Mills 7
Guy not out	42—	b Hillyer 22
Kynaston esq c Pilch	6—	b Hillyer 22
Lillywhite c Adams	7—	s Wenman 10
Cobbett b A Mynn	3—	s Wenman 7
Thackeray esq s Wenman	9—	not out 11
Byes 9 Wide 1 no b. 1 Total 119		Byes 10 W 2 n b 2 110

KENT

R Mills s Box	10—	c Sampson 0
W Mynn esq not out	26—	s Box 0
E. Wenman, b Cobbett	27—	c Kynaston 6
Pilch c Cobbet	3—	c Sewell 16
Hillyer b Redgate	9—	leg b wicket 0
A. Mynn esq c Cobbett	48—	b Redgate 29
Adams b Redgate	1—	b Redgate 0
C. Whittaker esq s Box	0—	b Redgate 9
Baker esq run out	12—	not out 7
W. Dorrinton, c Redgate	0—	not out 6
Martingale c Guy	4—	0
Byes 7 Wide 3 Total 150		Byes 4 Wide 3 80

Windsor, Printer, Cricket Ground, MALLING
Umpires—Messrs. Dean & Bailey.
A Dinner on the Ground at Three o'Clock.

The scorecard of Fuller Pilch's final first-class match at Town Malling in July 1841. Four further first-class matches were played here after Pilch's time, with the last being in 1890.

Chapter Seventeen
The birth of Canterbury Cricket Week

Many of the leading figures in the world of cricket had made their way to Canterbury for the third Kent match with England in 1841, including Benjamin Aislabie (the MCC secretary) and Lord Frederick Beauclerk (who had been MCC president in 1826), and all had been so impressed by the location and organisation that it was agreed to repeat the fixture the following season, plus a three-day, all-amateur version to follow. This encouraged John Baker and his brother William, who had appeared in the Kent eleven in all three matches against England, to suggest to the England captain, the Hon Frederick Ponsonby, that next year he should ask some of his undergraduate friends from his Cambridge University days, with whom he had formed a university amateur dramatic society, to come to Canterbury during the matches to provide entertainment at the theatre in Orange Street in the evenings. The gentlemen actors were delighted to be invited and in due course persuaded some professional actresses from London's West End to join them.

Details of the arrangements for a week of cricket at Canterbury in 1842 were released in May:

> Two grand matches on the 1st and 4th of August (Kent *v* England, and Gentlemen of Kent *v* Gentlemen of England) will probably occupy the whole week, and will be the most attractive matches in the country during the season. Amateur Performances will take place at the Theatre, Canterbury, with the assistance of Mrs Nisbett, Mrs Glover, and Miss Mordaunt. There will be a County Fancy Ball on the Wednesday, and a City Ball on the Thursday, at Barnes's Rooms.

But there was going to be a great deal more cricket played before August. Fuller's first match of the season was at Lord's on 20 and 21 June helping MCC beat the North by 43 runs. Redgate's haul of five wickets in the first innings and four in the second did not include Fuller's on this occasion. Kent opened their season against Sussex at the new Beverley Ground in Canterbury on 30 June, 1 and 2 July and won by four runs after Fuller had top-scored with 28 out of 80 in their second innings. There was still time for Fuller to take a quick trip to Brighton to help Chalvington beat the Brighton club by six wickets, thanks to his unbeaten 41 out of 93 in the second innings, and then go up to Lord's to join Kent against England on 11 and 12 July. The result of this match confirmed, if proof was still needed, that Kent were the champion county of cricket. *The Times* left its readers in no doubt:

The birth of Canterbury Cricket Week

There never was perhaps in the annals of cricketing a greater triumph than the one achieved on Tuesday evening at Lord's, by the players of Kent in their match with eleven selected from the various counties of England, and in which they, after two days of unrivalled play, were proclaimed the victors by a majority of no less that 50 runs. The England cricketers were unquestionably the finest in the world, and the 'Men of Kent' having now defeated, and without much difficulty, the elite of the gentlemen and professional players of this country, they are fairly entitled to the distinction of being styled the champions of the players of this fine game. For some past this match has been the principal topic of conversation among the members of the metropolitan, suburban, and provincial cricket clubs, and consequently a speculative interest has been excited. Indeed, bets to an immense amount have been pending on the result, and some idea may be formed of the anxiety with which that was regarded by those amateurs and players unavoidably absent and living in distant parts from the fact, that pigeon and horse expresses were dispatched after each innings, communicating the state of the game. The weather being propitious on both Monday and Tuesday, the enclosure at Lord's presented a gay and animated appearance from the immense assemblage of spectators, more than four thousand of whom paid for admission. There were above 100 of the equipages of the nobility and other distinguished persons, including a number of the carriages of ladies of rank and fashion.

Of the match it was reported that the bowling of Alfred Mynn, who took eleven wickets 'was universally admired', and his batting, top-scoring in both innings with 21 and 33 'was also very fine. His brother, Mr W.Mynn, Mr Felix, Mr Whittaker, and Pilch likewise displayed some pretty batting.' As 'pretty' as Fuller's batting may have been while scoring 10 and 21, it was ended in both innings yet again by Redgate.

Two days later Kent were at Brighton for an easy victory by ten wickets over Sussex, thanks to 53 from Felix, 46 from Fuller and 42 from Adams, and then Fuller was back at Lord's for the popular Fast Bowlers *v* Slow Bowlers match. He was moved back where he belonged into the Slow Bowlers eleven, but avoided being dismissed by Redgate on this occasion. Fuller was back in Sussex helping Chalvington beat Brighton again on 21 and 22 July. The last important match before Kent met England at Canterbury was the Gentlemen *v* Players annual challenge at Lord's towards the end of July. Unless of course, you count the one-day match between the 'Gentlemen of Rugby' and Kent at Lord's, as recounted by Harry Flashman in the sixth package of memoirs edited and published by George MacDonald Fraser in *Flashman's Lady* in 1977. There is no scorecard of that game in *Scores and Biographies* and the account of Flashman's hat-trick – Felix and Mynn bowled, Pilch caught and bowled – may be inventions of Flashman's creative imagination. What does ring true however, is his description of Lord's as he walked out to bat for the first time: 'the coaches were banked solid, wheel to wheel, crowded with ladies and gentlemen, the whole huge multitude hushed and expectant while the sun caught the glittering eyes of thousands of opera-glasses and binocles.'

Interest in the Gentlemen and Players game at Lord's had been steadily declining as the gulf in standards between the two sides continued to be as wide as ever and the result never in question. The proprietor of Lord's, James Dark, was unwilling to continue to lose money as paying customers stayed away and for the previous two years the matches had only taken place because Frederick Ponsonby, C.G.Taylor and Charles Bowdler had found ways to meet most of the expenses. But the 1841 game had been the closest for years and it seemed that the bad days were over and there would be no more talk of the fixture being abandoned. A big crowd turned up for the 1842 game. *The Times* reported that the 'ground each day was crowded with spectators, but at the Pavilion we missed several sporting noblemen and gentlemen, who usually attend the enclosure to witness great matches, and who, it appeared, were at Goodwood. There was, however, a good sprinkling of fashionables and an immense number of the Marylebone and other fashionable clubs.' The Gentlemen had not beaten the Players, when meeting on even terms, for 20 years, but at last the cycle was broken and they won by 95 runs. The Kent amateurs Felix and Mynn were the stars of the match, putting on 99 runs together in the Gentlemen's second innings before Mynn fell to Lillywhite for 46 and Felix was eventually caught at cover for 88 with *Bell's Life* noting 'some of the finest hitting ever witnessed.' Needing 163 runs to win the Players collapsed while only Fuller Pilch, 'esteemed as one of the finest batsmen of the country', could cope with the bowling of Mynn. As wickets fell around him, Fuller defended his stumps for as long as he could but was unlucky to be run out by some brilliant fielding after scoring six, and with him gone, all hope for the Players faded.

Fuller just found time to fit in yet another game for Chalvington at Brighton on 29 and 30 July and then dash back to Town Malling to enjoy his Sunday day of rest before leaving for the start of the very first Canterbury 'Cricket Week'.

Canterbury was buzzing with excitement. All the hotels and lodging houses in the city were packed with visitors. The owners of estates nearby had taken the opportunity to fill their country houses with fashionable guests earlier than usual so that they could enjoy the novelty of 'big-match' cricket and its associated entertainments during the days before the established social activities of 'Race Week'. It wasn't long before everyone could see that the idea was a winner. The *Kentish Observer* was much impressed:

> Canterbury, during the last three days, has exhibited a scene of bustle and activity, quite unusual in this quiet region. Each day the Beverley Cricket Field has been crowded with spectators. At the theatre, the amateur performers, aided by the professional talents of Mrs Nisbett and Miss Jane Mordaunt, attracted fashionable and crowded audiences. 'Othello Travestie', with its broad humour, provoked peals of laughter

from the boxes, pit, and gallery. Last night, there was to be a fancy dress ball at Barnes' Assembly Rooms where, it was expected, several splendid 'tableaux' would be formed, not, perhaps, equalling those at Her Majesty's ball, but full of taste and elegance, no doubt. At the Palace Gardens, exhibitions of fireworks have taken place: so that, altogether, what with the 'Cricket Week', and the 'Race Week', which is to follow, Canterbury will have a fortnight of gaiety, worthy of her best days.

There was a crowd of 3,000 on the Beverley new ground on the first morning to see Kent win the toss and start batting. Fuller went in after two wickets had fallen, but Walter Mynn went next at 39 for three. Now Nicholas Felix joined Fuller; *Bell's Life* said they 'commenced such a style of hitting and fine play that we never on any previous occasion had the felicity of witnessing.' The pair put on 154 runs before Felix was caught at the wicket for 74. At close of play Kent were 237 for four with Fuller, 'at the top of his form', not out on 98. The scene was set the following morning, when another big crowd gathered early to celebrate the completion of an historic century, but he was out almost immediately, caught by Dean off Lillywhite, without adding to his score.

Kent collapsed after that, although their final total of 278 was expected to be more than enough to win the game. Years later though, Fuller remembered, for Fred Gale's *The Game of Cricket*, the confidence of their supporters: 'one of the Kentish farmers offered thirty pounds to one on Kent, and an officer at Canterbury took him four times over.' But there were still plenty of runs left in the Beverley wicket and when Kent came to bat again, they had a lead of only 12 runs. Lillywhite took advantage of some poor batting, only Emilius Bayley reaching double figures in Kent's total of 44, and England went on to win by nine wickets. Fuller sadly recalled the disappointment of the unlucky cavalry officer who had lost his wager: 'Old "top boots" did sigh when he went home for his canvas bag to pay up.'

In the second half of the week the Gentlemen of Kent avenged the county's earlier defeat by beating the Gentlemen of England by 173 runs. This was a strictly amateur match with no professionals permitted on either side, so Fuller was able to take an unusual week off at the height of the season, perhaps to enjoy some of the entertainments provided during the evenings of match days at the theatre in Orange Street. Sheridan's play *The Rivals* may have appealed to him or Colman's *The Poor Gentleman*, where important parts were filled by some well-known actresses alongside the amateur gentlemen. But it is anyone's guess what he would have made of the burlesque *Othello Travestie* 'being the most excruciating Comical Operatic Tragedy by any Comical and Pastoral Company of Tragedical Tragedians' where all the parts, both male and female were taken by amateurs, many of them players in both matches, with Charles Taylor, the noted Sussex batsman, as 'Desdemona (a striking beauty)' supported by a band conducted by Nicholas Felix.

I think it is safe to say that, whatever Fuller thought of the productions, he would certainly have appreciated the prologue before the first performance of the week, written and performed by the dramatist Tom Taylor wearing cricket clothes and addressed to the cricketers in the audience:

> Cricket's the only thing I know a bit about;
> Ten years my shins and knuckles have been hit about!
> But, hello! Who are those I see down there?
> Pilch, Lillywhite, and Fenner - I declare!
> How are ye all? Where men like you assemble,
> It's not a little that shall make me tremble,
> While I stand here as champion of cricket
> You mind your fielding - I'll keep up my wicket.
> You will stand by me, never mind your County;
> Cricketers are all brothers; such I count ye.
> Your cricketer no cogging practice knows,
> No trick to favour friends or cripple foes;
> His motto still is 'May the best man win',
> Let Sussex boast her Taylor, Kent her Mynn,
> Your Cricketer, right English to the core,
> Still loves the man best he has licked before.

The evening performances in the Orange Theatre would become a regular feature during all Canterbury's Cricket Weeks in the future and the amateur acting company would eventually become known as the famous 'Old Stagers'.

The Week ended on Saturday, 6 August and, encouraged by its outstanding success, both on and off the field, the powers behind Kent cricket held a meeting at the Fountain Hotel under the chairmanship of the Kent MP, William Deedes, to discuss the future. A resolution was taken to establish 'upon a more extensive scale, a Kent Cricket Club.' The first steps were taken towards achieving that objective by making arrangements for Fuller Pilch to leave Town Malling and transfer his residence to Canterbury, the third cathedral city he had lived in, to take charge of the Beverley ground. A copy of his contract remains within the archives at the St Lawrence ground and as it has never been published before, I include it here in full:

> 1 This agreement is to be understood according to its most apparent meaning.
> 2 The Beverley Club shall pay Fuller Pilch £100 for his services for the year 1843, commencing on the 1st of January and ending December 31st.
> 3 The same to be paid quarterly the first payment (£25) to be made March 31st 1843.
> 4 When Pilch plays from home he is to receive the same as other players when at home, £2 each match.
> 5 The ground to be in Cricket order by the 1st of May and to be kept so during the season (Rolled, mowed, beaten, watered, holes filled, turf

replaced etc according to usual custom) under the superintendence and at the expense of Pilch.

6 The expense of enclosing the field for matches shall be defrayed by the Club.

7 Should Pilch's services be requested for any match unconnected with the B.C.C., there will be no general objection to his playing except when such match shall interfere with the B.C.C. as to time or when such match shall detract from the interest of any proposed match of the B.C.C. In all cases the manager or managing committee shall be consulted on this point.

8 That Pilch will play in no match of any kind IN KENT either in the neighbourhood of Canterbury or elsewhere in the county for the benefit of any Publican or for any person or Club whatever except the Beverley.[9]

9 All gate money to belong to the B.C.C. That Pilch will during the season give all reasonable time to practise with the members of the B.C.C.

10 Should illness or accident prevent Pilch from fulfilling his agreement that some new arrangement be entered upon from the time of such calamity not affecting any previous payments and that some equitable and proportionate allowance be made for any proved expenses incurred by Pilch.

NB This agreement is for the mutual advantage of both parties that they both may be out of all doubt as to that is expected each of the other.

It was signed by Fuller Pilch and by four members of the Beverley Club committee, John Bayley, W.Augustus Munn, Wm Baldock and I.G.A.Baker.

Eventually, responsibilities at Canterbury would restrict Fuller's freedom to accept most of the engagements he was offered outside the county. Until then, he would continue to go as often as he could to where the money was on offer, as he had done every year since arriving in Town Malling in 1836. So he resumed his usual round of matches two weeks later at Leicester, playing for MCC against the North who had Alfred Mynn in their side to balance the odds. He then moved across to Nottingham, taking five players from the MCC team with him, Dean, Lillywhite, Ponsonby, Sewell and Hillyer, plus Mynn, to meet a team put together by the ambitious William Clarke on 22, 23 and 24 August. Initially, Clarke had thrown out a challenge to MCC to bring an England team to play Nottinghamshire at Trent Bridge for the first time. Marylebone were not interested, so Fuller, seeing an opportunity to put some extra cash in his pocket, had stepped up and said he could bring a team of his own good enough to represent England, and also arranged for Box, Wenman, Hawkins and Dorrinton to join the side. Clarke and his team were put firmly in their place by England winning by

---

[9] One of the signatories, I.G.A.Baker, noted on the document at this point, 'This wants explaining I think.'

ten wickets after some fine batting from Fuller with 60 and Mynn with 61. *Bell's Life* said of the pair that they batted 'in a style the most superb possible, and while they beat the best balls down, they punished most severely the wide ones.'

Then it was back south for one more game for Kent, at Bromley, against England on 25, 26 and 27 August; then another engagement for Sussex at Brighton against England, in a match played for the benefit of William Lillywhite on 29, 30 and 31 August. While they were in Sussex some of the England and Sussex players, including Fuller, took the opportunity to play some village cricket as given men for Midhurst and Duncton as well as moving further along the coast to Southampton to play in the Hampshire and England match on 5 and 6 September. Hampshire had no regular county side at this time and despite being aided by five England players, Lillywhite, Wenman, Barker, Guy and Fuller Pilch (who top-scored with 19 out of 67 in the first innings), they lost by an innings and five runs.

There was still time for two more games in Sussex when Earl Winterton engaged Fuller and some of his travelling companions to play for him at Shillinglee Park, a landed estate in the High Weald of West Sussex, against Brighton. Fuller made top score of 36 out of Shillinglee's second innings total of 83 to set up a victory that was denied by bad weather in the first match on 12 and 13 September. In the return, at Brighton a few days later, Fuller top-scored again with 53 out of 114 but bad weather again prevented a result.

Chapter Eighteen
William Martingell joins Fuller at Canterbury

The second Canterbury Cricket Week was announced before the start of the 1843 season as part of the Beverley Cricket Club fixture list. There were to be the same two matches as the year before, Kent versus England and the Gentlemen of Kent versus the Gentlemen of England. There would be two further 'Grand Matches' at other times, Kent versus Sussex and the Gentlemen of Kent versus Eton College. The club, still known as the Beverley Club, would play neighbouring clubs nearly every week without the participation of Fuller Pilch, except for matches designated as 'Club and Ground' against Leeds and Benenden.

Expectations were high. The *Kentish Gazette* forecast that 'the approaching season will doubtless prove the most attractive and splendid ever witnessed. Fuller Pilch has already become a resident at Canterbury, and the Beverley Ground is in the best order, and not to be surpassed by any in the Kingdom.' It added that the pitch is 'now under the superintendence of Pilch, undergoing all the needful preparation for the period when Kent's manly sons will enter the lists in amicable strife against those of other counties of England, for the laurels of cricket.'

Fuller's duties would also include providing practice sessions for club members, and it was decided to support him with a full-time assistant to lessen the bowling load. William Martingell seemed to be a suitable candidate. Fuller had first seen him in 1839 while acting as umpire in a Town Malling match at Mitcham and, in the absence of a regular Surrey county eleven to take advantage of his talents, the 19-year-old had moved to Kent the following year to hire out his services to any club that needed, according to *Scores and Biographies*, 'an exceedingly good round-armed bowler, rather fast.' He took seven Town Malling wickets when playing for Penshurst and later bowled Fuller Pilch himself in a Tunbridge Wells and Hastings match. They played together for Tunbridge Wells against Sevenoaks in 1841 where Martingell was employed for a season, and Martingell began playing regularly for Kent soon after. Still only 24 years old, he was the ideal choice to join Fuller at Beverley and he was engaged in 1842 for £60 a year 'as a resident bowler at Canterbury who, with Fuller, will attend on the Beverley ground daily, to afford the members an opportunity to practice.' The young man was delighted with his appointment. Denison said of this arrangement in *Sketches of the Players*: 'Martingell, like all others who have looked into and considered the science of the game, became a vast admirer of Pilch; and his sole desire at this period of his life appears to have been to be so placed as to fall under the tutorship of so able and brilliant an expositor and illustrator of the object of his adoration.'

There is no record of Fuller's residence in Canterbury at this time and it would be another eight years before the Census of 1851 pins him down. What is certain is that he would no longer have time to augment his earnings by serving as a landlord at a local inn. That was an occupation to which he would not return until retirement in 1855.

Spring 1843 arrived and the duo of Fuller Pilch and William Martingell concentrated on coaching the members for Beverley Club matches during May and June. Then it was time for them to play in the Club and Ground games at Leeds on 12 June and Swingate the following day against teams that included both Mynn brothers. Then Fuller went off alone to play for MCC at Lord's against Midland Counties on 19 and 20 June where he found himself facing given-man Alfred Mynn for the third time in a week. Then Fuller, Martingell and Mynn had to join forces for three games for Kent at Brighton, Lord's and Canterbury. To everyone's amazement Kent lost the first one in the last week of June, a victory for Sussex after ten consecutive defeats. Chasing 162 runs to win, the resolute batting of Fuller had almost turned the tide until he ran out of partners and finished on 34 not out, with Kent just 20 runs short. Fuller and Mynn faced each other for a fourth time at Canterbury on 6 and 7 July when an East Kent team met West Kent. At Lord's on 10 and 11 July, Kent struggled to beat England by three wickets, although Fuller top-scored with 37 out of 113 in the first innings. In the return match with Sussex, at Canterbury on 13, 14 and 15 July, order was restored and Kent won by 116 runs.

Fuller was soon back at Lord's for MCC against England on 17, 18 and 19 July, where he top-scored in MCC's second innings with 43 out of 160. Then it was back to Canterbury for a Club and Ground match against Leeds Park on 24 and 25 July, when an unbeaten 89 for Fuller, 'amid tremendous plaudits', saw Beverley home to an innings victory despite some fine bowling from Mynn. The *Kentish Gazette* said 'Pilch, the Kentish hero, defied all the efforts of that excellent bowler.' This was followed by the Gentlemen *v* Players match that began on July 31 and won again by the Gentlemen, this time by an innings and 20 runs, despite Fuller's top score of 43 out of 99 in the Players' second innings. At last it was time for the second Canterbury Cricket Week where the *Gazette* reported 'premises adjoining the ground have been obtained as dressing-rooms, and arrangements made for enclosing the ground on all match days of public interest, and admission tickets free issued only to the members and subscribers.' Refreshments were organised by the landlord of the Globe Tavern, which was also used as the club house. Enjoying these new facilities, Kent beat England by nine wickets on 7 and 8 August, thanks to another unbeaten innings from Fuller with 57 out of Kent's first innings of 152 and Mynn and Hillyer sharing 17 wickets.

On 11 and 12 August Fuller was in Sussex to play for Lord Winterton's Shillinglee side against the Brighton Club in Brighton. Then it was back to

Kent where the Kent and England teams re-assembled at Thomas Hodges' ground in Hemsted Park for a match played on 17 and 18 August for the benefit of Ned Wenman, with the expenses of the England eleven paid by MCC. Large crowds attended thanks to the South-Eastern Railway making an extra stop at Staplehurst where coaches were available to transport spectators to and from the ground. Three days later Fuller arrived in Leicester for the return Midland Counties and MCC match. He did not play again until the benefit match for Thomas Box at Brighton between Sussex and England on 11, 12 and 13 September.

The 1844 season at Canterbury began with a very unusual event. This was a three-a-side single-wicket challenge on 24 May between Fuller and Martingell, each supported by two Beverley club members, with William de Chair Baker as one of the umpires. There were probably wagers on the result between club members as it was contested very seriously indeed. Fuller's team, 'The Lions', received 311 balls; they scored 16 runs, half of them by Fuller who received 151 balls, but added only two more runs off 39 balls in their second innings. Martingell's team, 'The Crowns', struggled to make a game of it with only three runs from 138 balls in their first innings and eight runs from 84 balls in the second.

Fuller's first double-wicket match of the season was at Lord's on 10 and 11 June, when he was engaged by Surrey and joined Martingell to help them to a three-wicket victory over MCC. Soon after his return from Lord's, Fuller was playing at Canterbury and demonstrating how the relationship between the Beverley Club and their neighbours at the Barracks was a benefit enjoyed by both parties. The officers of the 1st King's Dragoon Guards, subscribers to Kent Cricket Club, had according to the *Kentish Gazette* 'a field day under the superintendence of Captain Scott, seconded by the veterans Pilch and Martingell. The two elevens were completed by the permission of Colonel Hankey, and some excellent playing was exhibited.' Martingell appeared in Captain Cleaver's team while Fuller opened for the team under the joint leadership of Captain Scott and Captain Newland, scoring 45 out of 125, giving the cavalrymen a lesson in batting.

Fuller's next appearance was at Lord's when he joined Mynn, Wenman and Martingell to play for a West of England eleven against MCC on 24, 25 and 26 June. Then it was time for the usual short group of Kent matches, losing again to Sussex at Canterbury by one wicket despite Fuller's top scores in both innings, 38 out of 90 and 45 out of 107. Kent returned to winning ways beating England at Lord's on 1, 2 and 3 July. Fuller fitted in another appearance at Lord's on 8, 9 and 10 July, this time for Hampshire against MCC, where another unbeaten top score of 35 out of 90 could not save his team from defeat. Then he joined Kent at Brighton on 11, 12 and 13 July where they beat Sussex by nine runs.

There was still time to fit in another five games before Canterbury Cricket Week. Astonishingly they were for five different teams: for MCC against The North at Lord's on 15 and 16 July; for Norfolk, in their first appearance at Lord's since 1831, against MCC on 25 and 26 July, with victory for the county largely due to Fuller's 41, top score of the match; for the Players against the Gentlemen at Lord's at the end of July; for Buckinghamshire v Berkshire at The Brocas at Eton and finally a longer trip west to Bath to play for the West of England.

Kent's season ended with disappointment in the Cricket Week, losing to England by 52 runs despite Fuller's 13 out of 37 in Kent's second innings in a match that, due to the weather, took four days to complete between 13 and 16 August. But despite the weather it was another occasion when the proximity of the cavalrymen to the cricket ground paid dividends. Fred Gale described, in *The Game of Cricket*, the increase in fashionable ladies attending matches in Canterbury: 'The ladies look very charming when they walk about the ground between the innings, and the playing space is not curtained in any way, as the officers are kind enough to pitch their tents and keep the fair sex amused out of the way of the bowler's arm, and cricket is no way sacrificed to fashion.'

Then it was time for Fuller to take a short tour with MCC to play Sussex at Brighton on 19, 20 and 21 August, where 830 runs were scored in three days. *Scores and Biographies* thought this 'the largest number of runs that had been as yet made since the introduction of round-armed bowling.'[10] Fuller then went to play in the inaugural match at the New Ground adjoining Petworth Park in Sussex on 22 and 23 August, between Petworth and MCC, sponsored by Lord Winterton, and then made a longer journey to Leicester for the return match against The North on 26 and 27 August. Only two days later he was down at Southampton, to play with Mynn and Box for Hampshire against MCC, where his first innings score of 33 out of 107 kept them in the match so that they could go on to win by five wickets with Fuller making the winning hit. Then it had been time to go back up to Norfolk for the return match at Swaffham against MCC on 5 and 6 September. Fuller then travelled to Nottingham to play for the Gentlemen of Nottingham with Mynn against the Players of Nottinghamshire on 9, 10 and 11 September, where Fuller's 50 in the first innings was top score of the match, while he avoided being one of Redgate's seven victims.

It seems that Fuller had quickly learned how to use the advantages of the new railway system because only twenty-four hours later he walked on to the Racecourse Ground at Tunbridge Wells in Kent to play in a Married v Single match put on for the benefit of all the professionals. Perhaps this frenzy of travel back and forth between north and south, east and west, had disagreed with Pilch after all, because *Scores and Biographies* recorded 'Pilch was very unwell in this match.'

---

10 A total of 851 runs were scored over five days in the 'incomplete' match between Yorkshire and Norfolk at Sheffield in July 1834, referred to in Chapter Eleven.

Chapter Nineteen
William Pilch joins Uncle Fuller at Canterbury

There is no record of just how ill Fuller Pilch had been at the end of the 1844 season. However, it seems to have been serious enough to sound warning bells about the welfare of the famous, if not 'the most famous', cricketer in the country. There were always other players able to keep an eye on him when he was playing cricket in the summer, and staff, customers and friends would have seen him every day behind the bar of the inns where he had been engaged as landlord when he was not playing. Now he was in Canterbury living alone and his only out-of-season occupation was caring for the Beverley Ground where there was little to do during the autumn and winter months. Even his assistant William Martingell had temporarily moved away to work for the Earl of Ducie, a former MCC president, in Gloucestershire. He could have devoted his energies to developing his old profession of tailoring, if his accommodation was suitable, but that would do nothing to provide company out of business hours. Someone must have suggested, perhaps one of those who had invested reputation and money in getting Canterbury Cricket Week up and running as an attraction for the fashionable aristocracy of south-east England, that the 41-year-old bachelor needed someone to move in with him as companion and friend. Or at least someone prepared to share a house with a man known for his taciturn manner. A relative familiar with his personality would be ideal and, as luck would have it, there was a potential candidate. His nephew William was already a practising tailor and, at 23 years of age, an experienced cricketer for Norfolk.

Whoever decided to make contact with William and put the proposition to him, certainly had found the perfect answer. Over the next 12 years Fuller played some of his best cricket, while William earned a regular place in the Kent team, established a successful tailoring business in Canterbury, married a young Norfolk girl called Hephzibah at Walsingham in 1846, and had a son, Alfred, two years later, creating the ideal family home for his uncle. Their relationship would be celebrated in 1849 as part of a poem 'The Cricketer's Alphabet', published in *Bell's Life*, where it refers to the letter 'P':

> It also introduces Pilch, some call the Kentish Lion;
> And William Pilch, his nephew, and a very worthy scion,
> So mild and unassuming is the latter, sure I am
> They ought to designate the pair 'the Lion and the Lamb'.

Their first game together was a Club and Ground fixture for Beverley, now called the Kent Club, against the South London Club at the Beehive Ground in Walworth on 27 May, when William impressed with his bowling taking six wickets. Another player to impress was the young amateur Frederick Gale whose 33 not out in Kent Club's first innings was the highest individual score of the match. This was the same Frederick Gale who many years later would be the author of *The Game of Cricket* in which he wrote: 'I knew Fuller Pilch very well from the year 1845, when he coached us at the Beverley Ground at Canterbury', and described the sessions:

> Once and oftener twice a week we had a practice wicket and two professional bowlers from four o'clock till dark. The nominal price was 7/6d, but with odds and ends it amounted, perhaps, to 12/-. Any rising amateurs or lads of the village could try their hands at bowling under the direction of a professional, with sixpence on the wicket for the village lads, and at fielding at such places as short-slip, point, mid-off, etc. We generally got three gentlemen to come, so it cost about 4/- apiece, and we had a real enjoyable cricket afternoon - for it was strict practice, and furnished us with recruits when there was a vacancy in a good match.

When it came to organising the Beverley Club matches, Gale also remembered that Fuller knew ways of earning a little extra bonus:

> He used to make the match and captain the eleven; that is, he would tell us that a regiment or club wanted a match, and would play the Beverley if he could get an eleven to go, and recruits came in quick enough, and most charming matches they were. Sometimes there were off-hand matches at home, commencing at 2 o'clock, and there was no dinner, but simply a booth with sandwiches, bread and cheese, and a bit of cold beef for any who wanted it; but the cricket was real and true, and we had the old-fashioned six-ball overs in these matches; and every match with Pilch as captain was a lesson. On one grand occasion Fuller dropped an easy catch, and remarked in his dry way, 'I dropped her A-PURPOSE to teach you young gentlemen that cricket is a game of chance, I thought, LIKEWISE, as it is now September, that Mr Blank [whom he had missed] might send me some birds or a hare in hopes I might drop him another time.'

Gale had a taste of top-class cricket when he made his debut for the full Kent eleven a month later but was dismissed for nought and never played for the county again.[11] William Pilch, on the other hand, made his full debut for Kent that summer when he and his uncle travelled to Nottingham together, and he would eventually earn a regular place for the next twelve years.

---

11   Gale played for the Gentlemen of Kent at Lord's later in the season in a match now also recognised by ACS as first-class. Batting in the tail, he scored 13 and 0. His average in his two first-class matches was thus 4.33; he did not bowl. A better writer than player, you might say. The *Wisden* almanack of 1905 gave him a fulsome obituary of some 400 words.

Before the Kent season got under way, Fuller had four engagements to fulfil, including three at Lord's. There were very few runs scored in the first MCC game of the summer against Sussex on 2 and 3 June and it had taken nine 4-ball overs for Sussex even to open their account before collapsing all out for 49. Fuller made 12 in the MCC reply, the only batsman to reach double figures in a total of 68, and hit the winning run in the second. His next game was for Gravesend at home to Bearsted on 9 and 10 June, and then he returned to Lord's to play against MCC for the Western Counties on 16, 17 and 18 June, this time finishing on the losing side. The other game at Lord's five days later ended with an innings defeat for MCC against the North, a team that included the 19-year-old George Parr, who would eventually replace Fuller as the best bat in England, and who was making his debut at Lord's.

It was a poor season for Kent, who lost five of their six matches. Only Nicholas Felix, with 192 runs from eleven innings, and Fuller, with 150 from his eleven, made any significant contribution with the bat. It started off well with an innings victory over Nottinghamshire at Canterbury on 26 and 27 June, although Fuller was bowled by Redgate for only seven. A week later they went down by three wickets to Sussex at Brighton, despite Fuller's top score of 54 in Kent's second innings. Although no longer attached to a club in Kent, Martingell was allowed to play for the county in this match. Then Fuller and Martingell left the Kent team to join Hampshire at Lord's against MCC on 7, 8 and 9 July where not even Fuller's unbeaten 55 out of 141 in the first innings could save the visitors from defeat. Leaving London immediately after the end of the game, a Kent threesome were in Liverpool the next morning where Fuller was engaged to play for a Liverpool eleven and Martingell for a Manchester eleven that also had Felix as a given man. This was a unique match in which the first innings of each side was played at Liverpool and the last two at Manchester, taking three days on 10, 11 and 12 July. Martingell had Fuller caught by Felix in each innings for nought and four – so much for respect! The experiment of playing home and away in the same game, taking advantage of the new railway lines built between cities, does not appear to have found favour as it was not repeated anywhere else.

Fuller, Martingell and Felix immediately returned to London to face one another again at Lord's on 14, 15 and 16 July, where MCC had selected an England Eleven that beat Kent by 80 runs. Martingell, playing for England, caught Fuller in the first innings and bowled him in the second! Fuller, his nephew William and the Kent team were on a train as soon as the game ended to appear against Nottinghamshire at Trent Bridge on 17 and 18 July. Relieved perhaps not to be facing his friend this time, Fuller did everything he could to save Kent from defeat, remaining unbeaten on 29 out of 86 in the second innings chasing 65 to avoid an innings defeat but Nottinghamshire went on to win for the loss of only two wickets.

There were two Gentlemen v Players games in 1845, the traditional fixture at Lord's over four days in July and a benefit for George Brown, the Sussex

William Pilch joins Uncle Fuller at Canterbury

The well-known picture of the match between Kent and the England eleven, played at the old Beverley Club ground, then on the edge of Canterbury, in early August 1845.
(Courtesy of Canterbury City Museum)

heavyweight cricketer – like Fuller he was variously tailor and publican – at Brighton in September. Fuller top-scored in the Players' first innings at Lord's with 44 out of 127 and the Players won by 67. Next came the annual visit of Norfolk to face MCC at Lord's on 28 and 29 July, but William did not join his uncle in London, perhaps too busy with setting up their tailoring business in Canterbury. Fuller's top score, 22 out of 83, in Norfolk's second innings failed to prevent an innings defeat. Another defeat for Kent followed, losing by just seven runs to Sussex at Tunbridge Wells at the start of August and their decline continued in the Cricket Week match at Canterbury on 4, 5 and 6 August, losing to England for the second time that summer, despite Lillywhite being 'disabled and unable to bowl', according to *Scores and Biographies*. The defeat did not deter Fred Gale from enjoying the occasion as usual, particularly on Ladies Day, 'when the beauties of Kent come in swarms; and it doesn't matter if they sit with their backs to the game, and have a picnic with the officers and listen to the band. They look very charming.'

With no further engagements for Kent, Fuller went on his customary travels for the rest of the season. At Brighton in the second week of August he was in the MCC team that lost to Sussex who were without the injured Lillywhite, but then changed sides at Bath to play for the West of England, with Mynn and Box, on 18, 19 and 20 August, to beat MCC who had six players from the previous match, by an innings and 94 runs, thanks to 117 runs from Fuller. *Scores and Biographies* reported this as his tenth recorded century in cricket, adding 'though he may have made others!!'[12] Still recovering from his injury, Lillywhite failed to take any wickets, an unusual event for that great bowler. One day later MCC were at Southampton to face Hampshire who had engaged Fuller again. Lillywhite began to recover his form and took three wickets, although not Fuller, who contributed only nought and three as the hosts went down by 138 runs. Five of the MCC eleven plus Fuller then rushed off up to Nottingham to join five other members to play against the North on 25, 26 and 27 August, and win by 85 runs. Redgate had Fuller caught for four in the MCC second innings.

Earlier that year William Clarke had challenged Fuller Pilch again to bring his own 'England' eleven to Trent Bridge, and wagered £200 on the result. With neither Mynn, Lillywhite or Felix available to play, Fuller cobbled together an eleven from members of the MCC team that had played at Nottingham a week earlier, plus Martingell and Box who came up from London. Fuller tried to make a fight of it by top-scoring with 25 out of his England eleven's first innings of 95 to take a small lead, but it had been agreed that Nottinghamshire could field 14 players and this gave them the winning edge after three days of play on 4, 5 and 6 September. Sam Redgate took seven wickets in the match but could not include Fuller among his

---

12 It was certainly his third and last century in a match now regarded as first-class. It contributed greatly to his season's total of 564 first-class runs, making him the leading run-scorer in the season, for the ninth (and last) time in his career.

victims in what would be the last time that they were on opposite sides. Despite his early successes Redgate dismissed Fuller only 17 times out of the 61 innings in which they faced one another.

Before returning home, Fuller stopped off at Swaffham to appear for Norfolk who lost by an innings to an MCC 'touring' side on 11 and 12 September, and then travelled down to end his season at Brighton in the Gentlemen v Players benefit match for George Brown. There, captaining the professionals (perhaps the first time he had led a side in a first-class match), he was well set with an unbeaten 22 and the Players 119 for three on the first day of the match, September 15, when bad weather prevented any further play and the match had to be abandoned.

Chapter Twenty
William Clarke creates the All-England Eleven

In the spring of 1846 William Clarke moved from Nottingham to London to take up employment at Lord's as a ground bowler for MCC members. This placed him in the perfect position, when the MCC season finished at the end of July, to approach players to suggest they join his travelling team to tour the unfashionable but prosperous North of England to take advantage of the rapidly increasing railway network and the industry that had sprung up around it, as described by Charles Dickens in *Dombey and Son*: 'There were railway hotels, office-houses, lodging houses, boarding houses, railway plans, maps, views, wrappers, bottle, sandwich-boxes, and time-tables; railway hackney-coach and cab-stands; railway omnibuses, railway streets and buildings.'

Clarke intended to take his squad around the country to towns and cities where big-match cricket had not yet been seen, playing against teams of up to twenty-two local players. Using the title 'All-England Eleven' in order not to upset his masters at MCC who had traditionally managed and paid expenses for previous elevens to represent 'England' when asked to do so, Clarke expected to profit from the interest the games were sure to create. In a conversation with James Dark, the proprietor of the Lord's ground and manufacturer of all forms of cricket equipment, the confident Clarke declared to James Pycroft, who duly reported in *The Cricket Field*: 'It is a-going to be, Sir, from one end of the land to the other, you may depend on that; and what is more, it will make good for cricket – it will make good for you as well as me: mark my words, you'll sell cart-loads of your balls where you used to sell dozens.' But cricketers would need not only balls, but bats, hats, shirts, trousers, boots, gloves and leg-guards and it is no surprise that Clarke's ideas grabbed the interest of Fuller Pilch who saw opportunities to expand his own cricket equipment business, and when the time came he was ready to sign up for the tour.

But first there was a normal cricket season to play. Fuller and his nephew began their season playing for the Kent Club on 25 May at the Beehive Ground in Walworth, home of the South London Club. William's top score of 28 out of 72 in the second innings was not enough to avoid defeat by 41 runs. Three days later Fuller and Martingell were in the home side at Gravesend in an unfinished match against the Islington Albion Copenhagen Club which had hired Lillywhite, Hillyer, Dean and Dorrinton. The next day, 1 June, all six players were at Lord's for what was expected to be the most important match of the year.

Frederick Ponsonby had proposed to the MCC committee that a testimonial match for Nicholas Felix should be played in recognition of his services to the game. There was reluctance by some members to sponsor a match for the benefit of an amateur, even one who needed payment to cover his expenses every time he played, but as he was not an actual member of MCC, objections were removed. The committee selected the players who were to appear under the leadership of Felix himself, with Fuller Pilch in charge of the opposition and on the first day of the match at least 5,000 were attracted to St John's Wood. *Bell's Life* reported 'a vast number of influential gentlemen, patrons of and participators in the "noble" game, from almost every part of the country.' Just as many gathered on the second day, including Prince Albert who rode to the ground to see his first game of cricket, 'attended by some of the élite of the land' and was invited into the pavilion. He was so impressed that he stayed for nearly two hours. At the end of the first day, Fuller's side had a lead of 55 with eight of their second innings wickets in hand. When the next wicket fell on the second morning the lead was 73 as Fuller walked out to the middle. The final seven wickets went down for 87 runs while Fuller batted on to reach an unbeaten 31, including ten of the eleven runs scored for the tenth wicket. Despite the efforts of Parr, whose 59 was the highest individual innings of the match, Fuller's side won by 34 runs on the third day. *Bell's Life* thought it 'one of the finest matches ever witnessed.'

A week after all that excitement, Lillywhite, Hillyer, Dean, Dorrinton, Redgate and Fuller played in the return match between Gravesend and the Islington Albion Copenhagen Club on the ground next to the Copenhagen House Inn on 11 and 12 June. Fuller's top score in the Gravesend first innings, an unbeaten 34 out of 110, was never enough to save them from defeat by seven wickets. Six days later, on 18 June, a crowded Lord's was the scene of another epic encounter. The wealthy Banks brothers from Kent, William and Edward, were the backers of Arthur Mynn who had been challenged by Nicholas Felix for the 'Championship of England', with Edward Banks appearing as one of Mynn's two fielders. Felix failed to score from 15 balls in his first innings and after Mynn had hit five runs, Felix made every effort to overtake him by hitting 175 of the 247 balls he received, but the speed of Banks and his partner in the field kept his score down to a mere four runs and Mynn won by an innings. Fuller was not officially involved this time, nor in the return at Bromley in September, although he may have been present as he was not playing on either date.

Then it was time for the two contestants to accompany Fuller to Kent's first game of the season, against Surrey on 25 and 26 June at the Kennington Oval ground which had opened the year before. The two sides had not met since 1828 and the Surrey management were keen to establish a team that could compete with the other 'crack' counties. Taking advantage of strict qualification by birth, they were able to take Felix and Martingell out of the Kent squad and into their own on this occasion and beat their weakened opponents by ten wickets. A week later Kent came back strongly against Sussex at Brighton, beating them by 144 runs. On 6, 7 and 8 June William

Pilch played his first game at Lord's and Kent were unlucky to lose by one wicket when England's last man, Thomas Sewell, going to the middle with his team needing two runs to win, hit the first ball he received from Hillyer away to leg for the runs required. Fuller must have been disappointed that his top score of 27 out of Kent's second innings of 66 had not been a few runs more.

Fuller was absent from the Gentlemen v Players match at Lord's on 20, 21 and 22 July for the first time since 1829, for reasons unknown, but was able to join the Kent team when they met Surrey again at Preston Hall, not far from West Malling, on 23, 24 and 25 July. The ground was situated in the deer park where the local Aylesford Club had played from time to time. The owner, Charles Milner, now intended to establish a county club, to be called 'The New Kent Club', and play all future Kent matches against Surrey. In the park 'a well selected and spacious spot was fenced off for the accommodation of visitors' and a 'number of marquees' were erected for the first match. Fuller always enjoyed matches played in the grounds of private estates, telling Fred Gale: 'Ay, and haven't I seen some good company in many a butler's private room when we were playing a great match? Ay, and drink rare good stuff! The gamekeeper used to drop in by accident, and the ladies' maids and the housekeeper; and I have known some of the young gentlemen staying in the big house come down and smoke their cigars and talk cricket.'

Kent were lucky not to lose this game that ended as 'unfinished' after they had reached 29 for the loss of seven wickets, still needing another 43 runs to win. Their last two batsmen, the amateur brothers William and Edward Banks, had left the ground after rain had stopped play at 3 pm on the final afternoon as they believed that there would be no more play. Bad news for the brothers when it stopped raining and the match was resumed, but it was a remarkable piece of luck for the remaining nine of the Kent eleven who looked to be well beaten. Kent supporters of Messrs Banks and Banks may have argued that, as both were capable batsmen, Kent would have won if they had remained.

Two days later Fuller joined the Norfolk team at Lord's for their annual fixture against MCC on 27 and 28 July. He had arranged for Redgate to play for the county as a given man and the fast bowler rewarded the invitation by taking ten wickets in the match, although Norfolk went down by 88 runs. Two days after that Fuller was back with the Kent team that included Martingell once more as he had returned to his engagement with the Beverley Club, and they helped Kent beat Sussex at Tunbridge Wells. Then it was time for the Canterbury Cricket Week where, thanks to the completion of the South-Eastern Railway between London and Canterbury, even larger crowds attended. In another low-scoring match, with only 145 runs recorded over the two days, 3 and 4 August, England beat Kent by an innings and three runs. Only four Kent batsmen reached double figures in the match including Fuller with 15 before being bowled by John Wisden.

As the match had finished so early on the second day and the Gentlemen of Kent *v* Gentlemen of England match was not due to start for another two days, it was decided to fill the gap and entertain the spectators with a Gentlemen *v* Players challenge match. Seven of the Kent team including Fuller, and four from the England team formed the Players eleven and the Gentlemen included Felix, Edward Banks, Martingell and Lillywhite. There was time for only one innings each and the game was recorded as unfinished. Fuller avoided being one of Lillywhite's six victims but was bowled by Martingell for nought.

Two weeks later Fuller was in the England team at Brighton on 17, 18 and 19 August, facing Sussex in a second match played for George Brown's benefit. Before travelling north to join William Clarke in his new enterprise, there was time for the return match for Kent Club against the South London Club at Canterbury on 24 and 25 August. Fuller played an energetic part in the Kent Club victory by three wickets, taking six wickets and contributing 17 out of 45 in the Kent Club's second innings.

Fuller arrived in Nottingham on 27 August to play for an 'England Eleven' put together by William Clarke in a two-day match against 'Five Gentlemen of Southwell and Six Nottinghamshire professionals'. This put cash in Clarke's pocket to cover the initial expenses of his touring team booked to play three matches. Depending upon the fame of the player, his seniority and how well he performed in each game, Clarke was paying between £6 and fifty shillings (£2.50) for each appearance. Fuller signed up for all three games.

The first game, All-England *v* Twenty of Sheffield, on three days from 31 August at Hyde Park, Sheffield, was played according to the *Sheffield and Rotherham Independent* 'before the largest number of spectators, we believe, that ever assembled to witness a match since the making of the ground.' The *Independent* went on: 'From the well-known ability of the All England eleven, the names of whom had been for some weeks before the public, the interest, excited not only in the town and its immediate vicinity, but also amongst the lovers of this noble and manly amusement living at a considerable distance, was unusually intense. Parties in vehicles of every description, and groups of pedestrians, thronged our streets early during the mornings of the three days, and hundreds availed themselves of the advantages of railway accommodation.'

The locals won a low-scoring match by five wickets. Losing to Sheffield was not part of Clarke's script and Fuller's contribution of seven runs from his two innings may not have earned him the payment he was expecting. Top score of 62 at Manchester against Eighteen of Manchester on 3, 4 and 5 September, in an innings victory for All-England, should have redressed the balance and a win in the last of the three matches at Leeds against Eighteen of Yorkshire on 7, 8 and 9 September, would have left everyone satisfied although it began in controversy. The first five wickets of All-England fell for 15 runs, including Fuller for six, all to the bowling of

J.R.Ibbetson which was then declared 'unfair' and led to a change of umpires before the game could continue.

There was still time left for Fuller to move on to Norfolk to join the county against MCC on 10, 11 and 12 September. His 1846 season ended at Parker's Piece, Cambridge for Gentlemen of England against some old friends at the Cambridge Town Club who won by one wicket.

Chapter Twenty-One
The new St Lawrence Ground

In 1847 the Beverley Club acquired a field to the south-east of Canterbury that formed part of Winter's Farm on the Nackington Estate and gave up the ground next to the cavalry barracks. They agreed to pay an annual rent of £40 a year to the farmer who was a tenant of Earl Sondes and were delighted with their change of venue. The *Kentish Gazette* reported: 'It is situated an easy distance for the pedestrian from the heart of the city, and abuts upon the Old Dover Road, the ancient Roman Watling Street. The area is a park-like plot adjoining to, and part of the original pleasure grounds of St Lawrence House, the seat of the ancient Kentish family of the Rookes.' The house had fallen into disrepair and been pulled down at the turn of the century and the area grassed over before Fuller Pilch arrived to put the ground in order. As efficient as ever, he had it ready for an official opening on 16 May.

The club played its first game, with Fuller and William in the team, against Woodnesborough, who had Martingell and William Banks in their side. The *Gazette* said 'the company expressed themselves highly delighted with the ground, and the excellent accommodation offered them.' Marquees were available for hire and one was provided as a changing area for the gentlemen players. Fuller, William, and Martingell took advantage of the facilities at the Bat and Ball Inn, originally called the First and Last, just outside on the other side of the road. Then Fuller and the club team travelled up to the Kennington Oval to meet their old rivals, the South London Club, on 14 and 15 June and lost by an innings, scoring only 41 runs in their first innings (in which no player reached double figures) and 55 runs in the second.

Kent would not appear at St Lawrence until Canterbury Cricket Week and until then played six matches, winning five with the other ending in a very rare tie. They began with an innings victory over Sussex at Brighton on 24, 25 and 26 June, piling up a massive 259 runs, thanks to a century from Felix, 31 from Fuller and an unbeaten 27 from young William. Then two days later they were at Lord's for a win over England, thanks largely to an unbeaten 49 from Fuller in their second innings when wickets were falling quickly and they looked unlikely to present England with a difficult target. At Kennington Oval on 1, 2 and 3 July, Kent lost Felix and Martingell to Surrey again and the game swung backwards and forwards with first one side then the other gaining the ascendancy. When Kent came to bat in the last innings they needed 146 runs to win and after a top score of 36 from William and 24 from Fuller, the game looked won with Kent 145 for the loss of seven wickets. But the last three wickets fell without a run being added and the match was tied.

Directly after the Kent match at The Oval, Fuller renewed acquaintance with old friends from Bury and Suffolk at Lord's on 5 and 6 July, playing with them against MCC for the first time since 1831. Then he headed off down with William to Colonel Milner's Preston Hall for the return game with Surrey on 15, 16 and 17 July. This time there was no doubt about a clear result with Kent winning by exactly 100 runs, with Fuller top-scoring in the second innings with 26 out of 99. They both went straight back up to Lord's to appear in the Players eleven that beat the Gentlemen by 147 runs on 19, 20 and 21 July. Although veterans, William Lillywhite aged 55, who took eleven wickets, and William Clarke aged 48, who took the other nine wickets, claimed the credit, and William Pilch played an important part with top score of 32 in the Players first innings of 126.

It had been announced earlier in the season that James Dark was offering the use of Lord's ground for a testimonial in honour of Alfred Mynn. Everyone agreed that only a match between Kent and England would be worthy of such an occasion. MCC had appointed a special committee to supervise the arrangements, and it was reported that 'the Marylebone Club have adopted this plan to show the great esteem in which Mr A.Mynn is held as a gentlemen and as a cricketer, and there is no doubt but all cricketers, as well as the admirers of England's national game, will nobly respond to the call of their great leader at Lord's.' On 26 and 27 July most of the best players available turned out for England: Kent too were at full strength to win by seven wickets after two days during which, according to *Bell's Life*, was 'one of the largest assemblages ever witnessed congregated at Lord's, not less than 5,000 of the friends and supporters of Mr Mynn rallying round to give him honour.'

Two days later Kent were at Tunbridge Wells to beat Sussex again by 86 runs. And two days after that it was time to be at Canterbury for the Cricket Week and big-match inauguration of the new ground at St Lawrence on 2 August. The *Kentish Gazette* enthused:

> Marquees and pavilions, and refreshment booths, erected in different parts of the ground, forming a ring fence, the Union Jack and Royal Standard gaily floating in the breeze, gave a picturesque effect to the 'tout ensemble', and the appearance on those days when the company was most numerous it is impossible to adequately paint. The view produced an indescribable impression. Brilliant galaxies of Kent's famed beauties promenading or reclining in their carriages, the well-dressed beau, the moustached militaire, the commanding figures and noble mien of the representatives of Kent's ancient houses, the honest bluff countenances of the more staidly attired yeomen - all combined to perfect a scene only to be witnessed in merry England, and in which Kent is unsurpassed by any other county in the Kingdom.

A fictional match.
This is the key plate to the well-known lithograph of a 'match' played at Ireland's Ground, Brighton between Sussex and Kent in about 1847, showing Pilch with his contemporaries.
The figures shown, with Sussex fielding, are left to right: E.Napper (51), C.Hawkins (52), C.G.Taylor (53), J.Dean (50), T.Box (wk, 48), F.Pilch (batting, 47), J.Hodson (58), E.G.Wenman (46), F.W.Lillywhite (bowling, 44), W.H.Caldecourt (umpire, 45), J.Bayley (umpire, 56), Hon H.C.Lowther (56), R.Picknell (55), G.Brown and R.Cheeseman (scorers, 60 and 59).
St Peter's Church is in the background.

Inspired by this breathtaking atmosphere, Kent completed their season with a three-wicket win and claimed an unbeaten record.

After Canterbury Week, Fuller went up to Nottingham for the recently retired Thomas Barker's benefit match on 9, 10 and 11 August, and played in a very weak England team that lost by ten wickets. Then it was time to join Clarke's All-England Eleven at Leicester against Twenty of Leicestershire on 12, 13 and 14 August. But he was expected back at Canterbury for the East Kent Club and Ground return game with South London on 16 and 17 August and, before catching up with the All-England tourists, he also made a trip to Bury to play for Bury and Suffolk in the return game against MCC where he top-scored with 15 out of 49 in the second innings in a failed attempt to prevent an innings victory by MCC. Then he rejoined All-England for the game at York against Eighteen of Yorkshire on 23, 24 and 25 August, followed by four matches at Manchester, Birmingham, Liverpool and Sheffield between 26 August and 7 September against odds, respectively, of eighteen, twenty-two, sixteen and eighteen. Fuller didn't stay for the next fixture at Leeds starting on 9 September, deciding to break away to link up with his brother William on the same dates to help Norfolk beat MCC and made top score of the match in the first innings with 41, and then the second highest score in the second with 29 not out, facing Lillywhite and Hillyer at their best, who took 19 of the Norfolk wickets between them. This would be his last appearance for Norfolk for whom his career record in 21 matches was 886 runs with an average of 26.85, plus 44 wickets. It was also elder brother William's last game for Norfolk for whom he had appeared on 20 occasions, scoring 160 runs with an average of 4.40 and taken 56 wickets.[13]

After their match at Leeds, the All-England tourists had over a week to spare before their next game at Newcastle-upon-Tyne starting on 20 September. Viscount Milton invited them to spend it at his vast country house, Wentworth House near Rotherham. *Bell's Life* reported:

> A most joyous and a most English-like week it was; for, in the first place, whilst the hospitable board of the noble earl each day – it may almost be said each hour – groaned beneath every substantial delicacy of the season, so in the second was there so marked a personal attention on behalf of the members of the family towards them as was not merely extremely gratifying to all, but that at once convinced them they were welcome partakers of their lordships' munificence. Whilst the gentlemen of the Eleven [Mynn, Felix, Pell, Townley and Macawin] were received and regaled in the drawing and the dining-rooms with the family, the professional players had one of the large halls in Wentworth House appropriated for their use. Beds, too, were also set apart for each of the Eleven, the umpires, and the scorers under the roof of this splendid mansion.

Not surprisingly, Fuller rushed up from Norfolk to take advantage of the hospitality that was on offer. There was a lawn in front of the house, part of Humphry Repton's park landscape, which the magazine reported as '210 yards in length, and comprises between 14 and 15 acres of beautiful turf. This spot has been devoted by the noble earl to the purposes of cricket.' A match was arranged between a team captained by Viscount Milton himself, against a team captained by his brother the Hon Charles Fitzwilliam, splitting Clarke's squad between them and including some members of the Wentworth House club that had played there regularly. *Bell's Life* reported that, once the game got under way, 'Earl Fitzwilliam, and the Honourable Ladies Fitzwilliam, Lady Milton, and a string of company, occupied chairs upon the lawn, whilst there were a considerable number of visitors who ranged themselves around the scene of action.' Milton's side collapsed all out for 78 with Fuller unbeaten on 37. They had just avoided following on in reply to Fitzwilliam's 174 who then rattled up another 154 to lead by 250, but there was no time for Milton's side to bat again and the match was left unfinished.

Fuller and the All-England players then went off to play their match at Newcastle against Twenty of Newcastle followed immediately by a match at Stockton-on-Tees against Twenty-Two of Stockton and North Yorkshire. As soon as that game ended Fuller and half-a-dozen others, including

---

13 Eldest brother Nathaniel had retired three years earlier after scoring 267 runs with an average of 10.27 and taken five wickets in 15 matches for Norfolk.

Part of the well-known picture of 1847 by Nathaniel Felix, showing Fuller Pilch and colleagues in William Clarke's All-England Eleven. From left to right: J.Dean, N.Felix, O.C.Pell, W.R.Hillyer, F.W.Lillywhite, W.Dorrinton, F.Pilch and T.Sewell, sen.

Alfred Mynn, travelled 300 miles down to Brighton to appear in the last-ever match played on Box's Ground on 27, 28, 29 and 30 September.[14] Mynn played as a 'given' man for Sussex while the others appeared for England. Fuller top-scored with 39 in England's first innings but Sussex won by 27 runs. Then Fuller, Mynn, Martingell, Guy and Parr went back up to Stourbridge in Worcestershire for the last contract of the summer in Clarke's All-England Eleven against Eighteen of Stourbridge, with Hillyer and Box.

Fuller played nine times for Clarke that year and had agreed to serve on the All-England committee with Mynn and Hillyer. He made a few runs here and there, his highest score being 43 against Eighteen of Manchester. He managed to score 178 runs from his 16 innings, but George Parr, anxious to

---

14   This ground, also known as the Royal New Ground, Ireland's Gardens and the Hanover Ground (among others) off Lewes Road, Brighton staged 49 first-class matches between 1814 and 1847, 29 of them involving Fuller himself.

impress, made 404 runs from his 16 innings, and Felix made 266. It might seem that Fuller was only going through the motions as one of the star players hired to bring in the crowds. But it should be remembered that there very few gaps in a field occupied by 18, 20 or 22 fieldsmen and that Fuller, now 43, was not as fast between the wickets as he used to be. His offside style of batting meant that he was usually attempting to strike the ball past a point, cover point, an extra cover, a couple of deep covers, a 'middle wicket' and two long offs, as well as a third man, long slip and deep long slip. Parr, by comparison, was a strong leg-side batsman and an expert at finding gaps in the field on that side, even when it was more populated than usual.

Chapter Twenty-Two
Three cheers for the 'stale' men

The following year, 1848, Clarke decided to make an earlier start to touring with his All-England players and not wait for MCC to complete their programme. Fuller appeared twice for Clarke in June, against Twenty-Two of Birmingham at Edgbaston on 19 and 20 June and Twenty-Two of Worcestershire at Worcester on 22, 23 and 24 June. He came back to Lord's for Kent's first match of the season against England on 10 and 11 July, which they lost by 55 runs despite the efforts of Edmund Hinkly, making his debut at Lord's, who took six England wickets in their first innings and all ten wickets in their second, only the second time ever in a first-class match.

Fuller missed the next All-England match at Walsall and did not appear again anywhere until 27, 28 and 29 July when Kent lost to Sussex by one wicket at Tunbridge Wells. Two days later he was back at Lord's for the Gentlemen *v* Players match won by the Gentlemen by 27 runs. Fuller top-scored with 18 out of 79 in the Players' first innings. Then Clarke brought his All-England players into Kent and Surrey for the first time and played at Gravesend on 3, 4 and 5 August to beat Fifteen of West Kent by 21 runs, but lose by eight wickets to Fourteen of Surrey at Kennington Oval on 7, 8 and 9 August. Surrey had claimed both Felix and Martingell for their team, plus the Kent bowler Hinkly, who only qualified by a brief residence near to The Oval, and justified his engagement by taking eight wickets in the match, including Fuller's in the second innings.

Fuller rejoined Kent at the Hove ground on Brunswick Lawns for their return match with Sussex on 10, 11 and 12 August, which ended in a draw with Sussex on 23 for six, still needing another 15 runs to win. Kent won their last game of the season against England by ten wickets at Canterbury, on 15 and 16 August, thanks to a brilliant 54 from Fuller in Kent's first innings of 125 in which only William Pilch and William Dorrinton also reached double figures. Then Fuller caught up with Clarke's men at Coventry against Twenty-Two of Coventry on 17, 18 and 19 August, but missed the next game at Derby before playing again at Manchester against Fifteen of Manchester on 24, 25 and 26 August. He was taken ill during the game at Bradford against Eighteen of Bradford in the first week of September, and returned to Canterbury, missing the final seven All-England engagements.

He did not play again that season. It seems that age – he was now 44 – was beginning to catch up with him and in the views of some he was not alone. A letter appeared in *Bell's Life* on 30 July from a correspondent signing himself as 'A Member of a Metropolitan Cricket Club' complaining that players chosen to represent England and other important sides were of poor quality because too many of them were 'veterans', although he made an exception for the 57-year-old William Lillywhite:

> The gentlemen who select the elevens for the great matches seem to forget that, except in some very rare instances, (Lilly, for example, who is indeed a phenomenon), age must, will, and does tell, and youth must be served in cricket as in other matters, of which you know somewhat. Now, perhaps I shall make a good many cricketers laugh, and many more stare, when I say that, were I to select an All-England Eleven to beat any other Eleven in the world, I would not have either Pilch, Mynn, or Felix, and for this very reason – they are all three stale men. Great indeed have they been in their day – none greater in my somewhat limited recollection – but their time has gone by, and they can well afford to live upon their reputations without intercepting with the long shadows of their sunset other rising suns.

This led to a flood of letters in defence of the 'three stale men', one of them in verse:

> Three cheers for the 'stale men', they'll never say die
> Whilst a bat or ball they can wield;
> In truth we shall laugh, aye, and stare, if you cry
> That they ne'er should be seen in the field.

> Our Alfred the Great is full great as of yore,
> Aye, and Fuller, deny it who will?
> Though Felix's infelix oftimes in the score,
> Yet, 'in', Felix can show you some skill.

> Then talk not again of the deeds they have done,
> But speak rather of those they will dare;
> For backwards their 'sunset's long shadows' will run
> Till unseen in their noon's brilliant glare.

> Three cheers for the 'stale men', no 'freshmen', we say,
> E'er again such a trio will be;
> Nine cheers will much better their merits display,
> For they are themselves three times three.

Fuller certainly did not believe that his time had 'gone by' and instead of slowing down he appears to have taken new responsibilities in 1849 by coaching university undergraduates and developing the Prince of Wales Ground, off the Iffley Road in Oxford. Most of the colleges had their own sports fields and both University and Oxfordshire played at whichever one of these was available. Fuller may have been persuaded by ex-Kent colleague Edward Martin, who kept a cricket equipment shop in Oxford, and who came from a family of cricket-ball makers, that by providing superior facilities they could establish the official home for cricket in the city. Meanwhile, he went across to Cambridge to join the All-England

Eleven and play the Cambridge Graduates and Town Club on 21, 22 and 23 May, and then went straight back to Oxford where he had arranged for the Kent team to play Sixteen of Oxfordshire at the Prince of Wales Ground on 24 and 25 May, in preparation for their encounter with Yorkshire at Sheffield at the end of the month. The Kent players certainly needed the practice. They started their second innings twelve runs in front and then crashed to 36 all out with an unbeaten 16 from Fuller, the only batsman to reach double figures, and Oxfordshire won by ten wickets. After this wake-up call Kent recovered to beat Yorkshire by 66 runs three days later. The two counties would not meet again until 1862.

Fuller returned to Lord's to play in the Married *v* Single challenge on 11, 12 and 13 June, in which he and nephew William appeared on opposite sides and the Singles won by three wickets. One week later he was back at Lord's to play for the England team selected by MCC against Surrey, and then, playing for Kent with William at Gravesend on 21 and 22 June, he found more than half of the same England team in an All-England team put together by Clarke which was too good for Kent and won by 43 runs. Clarke then took eleven players from Gravesend to play Fourteen of Hampshire at Southampton at the end of June. Many of the All-England team, including Clarke and Fuller, now returned to Lord's on 9 and 10 July to play in either the England Eleven selected by MCC or the Kent team. Fuller made top score of 34 in Kent's second innings but England lost only three wickets before reaching the 58 runs they required to win. Kent's next match was against Sussex at Hove on 12, 13 and 14 July in which a remarkable total of 684 runs were scored, including 53 by Dean for Sussex and 92 from Alfred Mynn and 78 from Adams, as Kent went on to win by 116 runs. Fuller's contribution was only one and 35 but, in an attempt to stem the flow of runs, he was brought on to bowl and took three wickets.

MCC decided to revive the North *v* South match at Lord's in mid-July, the first such challenge since 1838. John Wisden played for the North, based on his residence at Leamington Spa. According to *Scores and Biographies*, he 'should not have done, as birth always counts before residence. The North, however, being considered weak in bowling, he was allowed to form one of that side.' The switch did not quite work out in the way that MCC had envisaged. Wisden, with seven wickets, and Clarke, with nine, proceeded to bowl the South out for 48 and 67, and the North won by 243 runs. Fuller was run out for two and caught off Wisden for six: Felix went first ball in both innings, first to Wisden and then to Clarke. Two days later Fuller made 52 and Felix 49 for the All-England Eleven at Hull to beat Twenty-Two of Hull by an innings.

Fuller and Felix returned to Lord's for the Gentlemen *v* Players match on 23 and 24 July. This would prove to be the last appearance by Fuller in this historic fixture, which on this occasion was won by the amateurs for the first time by an innings, thanks to some brilliant fast bowling by Harvey Fellowes, who took ten wickets in the match. He might have had eleven but Lillywhite had been hurt by Fellowes on the wrist and, according to *Scores and Biographies*, 'refused to go in.' Fuller did what he could to keep the professionals in the game with 24 out of 65 in reply to 192, and was the only Player to reach double figures, although the change in the Laws meant that they had to follow on and there was little improvement in their second innings with Guy reaching 25 and Box 26, out of a final total of 87. Felix had top-scored for the Gentlemen with 21 in their only innings and this must be a rare, if not unique, instance in an important match where a team has lost by an innings yet provided the three highest individual scores.

Clarke's All-England 'squad' now left for two engagements at Nottingham and Leicester, but Fuller did not join them until they reached his old ground at Bury St Edmunds to play Eighteen of Bury and Suffolk on 2, 3 and 4 August. Their old hero failed to attract the crowds of years before, although he even bowled twenty overs and took six wickets as a reminder of past glories, and attendance was disappointing over the three days 'for so great a display of the finest cricketers England can produce.' Two days later Fuller and most of the All-England eleven were at the Kennington Oval playing in the Surrey *v* England match. Then they all travelled down to the West Country to play Eighteen of Dorsetshire at Weymouth on 9, 10 and 11 August.

Kent had two more matches to play and won them both. They beat Sussex by 18 runs at Tunbridge Wells on 16, 17 and 18 August and then it was time for Canterbury Week where, on 20, 21 and 22 August, they made up for the two earlier defeats that year and beat England this time by 206 runs. Fuller made top score of 34 in Kent's first innings, making amends for the unfortunate dismissal of Nicholas Felix. The *Kentish Gazette* reported that 'with his score at seven Mr Felix was run out from too great an anxiety to add to his score. His co-batsman, Fuller – and where is there a better judge? – saw the hit did not justify his moving from his ground; but Mr Felix, not seeing that his ball went direct to "him at the slip", moved off, and 'ere he could recover his ground "his timbers were shivered".'

Only twenty-four hours later Fuller was in Warwickshire playing for the All-England Eleven against Twenty-Two of Atherstone and two days after that they were at Derby against Twenty of Derbyshire. Staying in the Midlands they went to Leamington where Wisden and Parr had established their own ground and would be hosts for the return match North *v* South at the end of August. Fuller's top score of 29 out of 87 in the South's second innings could not save them from another defeat.

He ended the season by playing six consecutive odds matches for Clarke in September, against sides representing Sheffield, Manchester, Leamington and District, Leeds, Stockton-on-Tees and Birmingham. Fuller only scored 124 runs in his twelve innings, but his highest score of 39 in the second innings of the last game played a major part in All-England's one-wicket victory to end the tour on a high note.

Chapter Twenty-Three
Fuller's final seasons

Between 1850 and Fuller's last appearance for them in 1854, Kent played 23 matches and lost 18 of them. They drew three and won only two - at Hove against Sussex in 1850 and at The Oval against Surrey in 1852. Fuller would later confess to Frederick Gale: 'The fact was we all grew old together and I often think some of us played a year or two too long; but then the truth was, though I say it, the public liked the names of Mynn and Felix and Wenman and Hillyer, Adams, Dorrinton, Martingell - ay, and of Fuller Pilch too. And I think we kept the candle burning a little too long.'

Fuller played in 20 of the 23 Kent matches and he continued to be Kent's leading run-scorer with 565 runs from his 37 innings, the next highest being Thomas Adams with 534 runs from 44 innings.

In 1850 Fuller continued with his development of the Prince of Wales Ground at Oxford, in partnership with Edward Martin. The pair had made great progress with ground improvements. The *Oxford Journal* reported that 'no expense has been spared to make it as perfect as its limited space will permit'. They were now making cricket bats at the ground, both the 'plain' match bat and the newer, spliced version,[15] trading as 'Fuller Pilch and Martin'. Fuller also concentrated on spring coaching for the undergraduates, missing four games for Clarke. But instead of bringing a Kent side this year, he used his influence to persuade Clarke to bring his All-England Eleven to play Eighteen of Oxfordshire on 16, 17 and 18 May, hoping to encourage further the development of cricket in the county. The *Oxford Journal* was impressed:

> The match excited considerable interest and attracted some hundreds of persons from this city and neighbourhood; and the ground, with its marquees, stands, and tents, presented the appearance of a fair. A capacious booth, well supplied with refreshments of every kind by Mr Greenwood of the Maidenhead Inn, afforded great accommodation to large numbers who gladly availed themselves of the good cheer within.

Encouraged by the atmosphere, Oxfordshire ran riot and won by 187 runs.

The All-England side went off to play three more games without Fuller, who returned home to concentrate on four consecutive matches for Kent

---

15 Spliced bats were introduced in the mid 1830s, according to Hugh Barty-King's book 'Quilt Winders and Pod Shavers', perhaps initially as 'the *haute couture* of the bat maker's art'. Many professional cricketers of this period were bat makers at some time in their lives. The Alfred Mynn bat made by Pilch and Martin, at one time on display in the Lord's museum, has no splice.

starting at Hove against Sussex on 17, 18 and 19 June. Fuller top-scored with 41 in the first innings and Kent won by five wickets. Rain prevented a result at Tunbridge Wells in the return with Sussex on 4, 5 and 6 July, although Kent would have needed 236 runs in their second innings to win the match after Wisden had scored 100 in the Sussex second innings. At Lord's on 8, 9 and 10 July, Kent lost to England by six wickets after Fuller had top-scored in the first innings with 49 out of 129. They then went straight to The Oval where Surrey slaughtered them by an innings and 110 runs. After nought in the first Kent innings of 52, Fuller had contributed 31 out of 84 in the second in an attempt to save the game.

There was a brief respite for Fuller from Kent's agony with an East Kent Club match at Canterbury against Stilebridge in mid-July, but then he was back with the county at Cranbrook to play Clarke's All-England Eleven. This was heading towards another defeat for Kent before time ran out with Kent on 44 for five chasing 131 to win, although Fuller had gone in to bat late and was not out with Mynn, Felix and Wenman still to bat. Fuller stayed with Clarke's squad to return to The Oval to play Fourteen of Surrey on 25, 26 and 27 July. Two days later it was another Young v Old challenge at Lord's for the benefit of William Caldecourt who had been a practice bowler for MCC for over thirty years.

Fuller missed the next two All-England matches in order to prepare for Canterbury Cricket Week. Kent played England on 12, 13 and 14 August and were set a target of 179 runs to win. While Harvey Fellowes was blasting down seven Kent wickets, Fuller put up strong resistance with 51 before he too fell to the sheer speed of the bowling and Kent finished 16 runs short. Instead of his usual engagements in Kent and Sussex, Fuller spent the rest of the summer playing for Clarke in nine odds matches, each of two or three days, between 26 August and 2 October, at Peterborough, Manchester, Sheffield, Darlington, Bradford, Malton, Hove, Louth and Birmingham. Fuller had continued to struggle making runs when faced by larger groups of fielders: his best score was 52 against Sixteen Amateurs of Sussex, but he made a mere 98 runs from another fifteen innings. However, the crowds continued to gather at most of these grounds with the expectation of seeing the 'great Fuller' at the wicket as well as Mynn, Felix and the new star, George Parr, while Clarke counted up the profits.

On 30 March 1851 there was another Census taken and this time we have confirmation of Fuller's residence and household companions in Canterbury. They are all living at Bridge House in Lamb Lane, close to the High Street and overlooking the Great Stour, a narrow river that runs through the city. Surprisingly, Fuller is not listed as 'head of household' as this honour is taken by nephew William who also indicates that his occupation is 'tailor'. Hephzibah is there as William's wife and Alfred as his son. They have taken in one lodger, a schoolmistress named Amelia Christopher and engaged 20-year-old Mary Ann Wilkinson as a live-in servant. First on the handwritten list, however, is Fuller, aged 47, with the occupation of 'bat-maker'.

```
PILCH, Fuller

PILCH, Fuller                                          M.49.10

    Bat of Fuller Pilch (1803-1870).

    Stamped on blade and top of handle:  F. Pilch

       Length:  35¼ ins;  blade:  22 ins.. 2 lb. 10 oz.
    Back humped/rounded transitional.   Face slightly convex.
    Unspliced handle.

    Attached:  Portrait of Pilch.

    Purchased from Mrs. C. Britton, 1949.
```

The Lord's museum record of a heavy, unspliced bat, apparently made and used by Fuller Pilch himself.

No doubt an increase in the membership of the East Kent Cricket Club had triggered off a demand for equipment of all kinds, especially bats, as it would have been fashionable for gentlemen and officers to have their own bats made to order. In the Kent County Cricket archives at Canterbury there is a receipt, signed by William, who seems to have been in charge of the paperwork, on Fuller's behalf, for £11 8s 6d for the supply of 'practice bats, balls, stumps and bails' in 1849 as well as a bill on printed paper headed 'F & W Pilch, tailors and drapers'.[16] At first sight it seems strange that Fuller preferred to label himself in the census as a manufacturer of cricket equipment rather than as a 'tailor' or 'cricketer', but with his playing days drawing to a close his thoughts may have been looking to the future. If he was going to be able to support himself during his retirement he would need to expand his business as a supplier of cricket accessories further than Canterbury and Oxford while his reputation was still big enough to attract new customers in what was becoming a very competitive market.

Not long after the census was completed, Fuller was back at Oxford, coaching as usual, in the spring of 1851, preferring to miss the first eight All-England games in May before joining them at the beginning of June for the next six, beginning against Twenty-Two of Wisbech and District. Clarke agreed to bring his All-England Eleven to Oxford again to play Sixteen of Oxfordshire on 6 and 7 June, but the development of the Prince of Wales ground by Fuller and Martin had been abandoned and they arranged for the

---

16   Fuller was certainly not illiterate, though there was no compulsory education in his time. I have found no record of his formal education other than a brief reference to his study of Greek at school. It is believed he grew up in Brisley, not far from his birthplace, and may have attended school there or at nearby Mileham which had a free school endowed in 1743.

match to be played at the new Christ Church Cricket Ground. The *Oxford Journal* reported:

> The match excited considerable interest and attracted a large number of spectators to witness it, for whom there was ample accommodation in the way of tents, stands, seats, etc. Mr Greenwood, of the Maidenhead Inn, was on the ground with a spacious booth, where 'creature comforts' were liberally dispensed, so that hunger could be appeased, or thirst quenched, in the most effectual manner, and at a moderate charge. In consequence of the proximity of this new cricket ground to the town, a large number of farmers and others from the country availed themselves of the opportunity of witnessing the play on Saturday.

The eleventh All-England match was played at Lord's on 9, 10 and 11 June, against Fourteen of Marylebone and is the only match where MCC played with the odds of more than eleven men. The match ended with controversy. All-England had been set 115 runs to win and, thanks to 50 from Fuller, reached 114 for the loss of five wickets. Then time was called and the match declared as unfinished with all bets drawn. *Scores and Biographies* later commented: 'Though the MCC were correct, strictly speaking, in drawing the stumps exactly at the time, and thus preventing England from winning, still it certainly was not cricket or sportsmanlike, and it created (at the time) quite an uproar.'

The next three All-England matches were against Fourteen of Surrey, a Twenty-Two at Banbury, and a Twenty-Two of Herefordshire, at Ross-on-Wye. Then Fuller headed for Kennington Oval for the North *v* South match on 3, 4 and 5 July, where he showed he had lost none of his old bowling skills by taking four wickets, including George Parr for nought, in the North second innings. Two days later he was at Lord's with Kent against England with top score of 22 out of Kent's first innings 52. It was a low-scoring match over in two days with no team innings reaching three figures and England won by seven wickets. Moving on to Hove to face Sussex on 10, 11 and 12 July, Fuller top-scored again with 54 in Kent's first innings, but it was not enough to prevent a Sussex five-wicket victory. A Kent Club match followed shortly after at The Vine Ground against the Sevenoaks Vine Club with Hillyer as their given man. Fuller and William shared all ten Sevenoaks first-innings wickets and Fuller followed this with an unbeaten 33 out of a first innings of 90. Sevenoaks eventually set a target of 204 but there was not enough time for the Kent Club to bat again.

Clarke brought his All-England Eleven to Cranbrook to play Kent on 24, 25 and 26 July. The whole of the first day was lost to rain and there was no time to finish the game. It was almost a disaster for Kent, however, when in reply to All-England's first innings of 122 they lost their first three wickets cheaply. Fuller and Wenman stayed in the middle together, determined to stop the rot, at one time remaining scoreless for 32 consecutive four-ball overs. In the end Fuller made 37 and Wenman 30 to ensure that Kent were only fifteen runs behind. All-England were all out for 84 in their second innings but there was no time for Kent to make a start on chasing the 100-run target.

The Young *v* Old match at Lord's on 28, 29 and 30 July was played for the benefit of John Bayley, a practice bowler for MCC since 1823: Fuller with his 'Old' companions won by seven wickets. Two matches for Kent came next. They lost to Sussex by 62 runs at Tunbridge Wells at the beginning of August and then went on to lose to England in Canterbury Week by four wickets on 11, 12 and 13 August, with Fuller making three scores in the twenties in these games.

There were no more Kent matches arranged that summer, so two days after Canterbury Cricket Week ended, Fuller went to Dorset to link up with the Clarke squad for eleven consecutive games between August 18 and September 24, travelling throughout England and Scotland to play odds matches, many of them of two or three days duration against Twenty-Twos, in places as widely separated as Sherborne, Worcester, Stoke-on-Trent, Ilkeston, Sheffield, Huddersfield, Bradford, Newburgh Park (near Aberdeen), Edinburgh, Glasgow, and Birmingham. It is said that at Glasgow, he cut he pitch himself, with a scythe, shortly before the match started.

Clarke then took his players off to Devon, Hampshire and Sussex without Fuller who returned to Norfolk to end his season with one of the most extraordinary innings of his career. The game took place over three days in October, the actual dates were not recorded, at Mr Springell's Field at King's Lynn in Norfolk, where his brother William had moved to take over as innkeeper of the Royal Oak. It featured the Lynn Club against Twenty-Two of Lynn who were strengthened by the inclusion of Fuller Pilch in their crowded ranks. Lynn Club made 96 in their first innings with Fuller, even at his age, showing everyone how to bowl by taking six wickets. The Twenty-Two managed to score 39, with only one batsman reaching double figures, and no, it was not Fuller; his contribution was nought! The Club managed 43 in their second innings, with Fuller taking another five wickets, and the Twenty-Two needed 101 to win. Once more only one batsman reached double figures, and this time it was Fuller. But what double figures they were! An unbeaten 70 runs to take his team through to a two-wicket victory.

The All-England Eleven began the 1852 season in Scotland on 10 May without Fuller and he did not play in their first five matches. His season began on 28 May at Canterbury in a one-day match for the Canterbury Club against the Manchester Club, who three days earlier had played MCC at Lord's, and were allowed John Wisden as a given man. Three days later Fuller joined Clarke's All-England Eleven at Lord's to play a combined Surrey and Sussex Eleven who won by 51 runs. Then the All-England Eleven, including Fuller, moved to the Kennington Oval to play Surrey on 3, 4 and 5 June. Fuller's contributions in these games were modest, two runs in four innings. In the second match Clarke switched sides to play for Surrey with Parr and Bickley, underscoring the unsatisfactory nature of the team names. Clarke then took everyone down to Chichester to play Sixteen of Sussex in another benefit match for the Sussex veteran George Brown, but play was only possible on June 8, the first and third days being rained off.

Fuller did not play in the next All-England game at Ipswich as he had taken his own All-England Eleven to Oxford on the same dates to play Sixteen of Oxfordshire on 11, 12 and 13 June at the Christ Church ground. This was well received in the *Oxford Journal*:

> The All-England side was infinitely superior to any previous eleven that had visited Oxford, and embraced an unusually large number of the most distinguished batters and bowlers in the kingdom. Great credit is due to Pilch and Martin, not only for the judicious selection of the side, but for their spirit and enterprise in getting up the match, by which they will be losers, in consequence of the wet weather keeping so many away who otherwise would have been present, and contributed by the payment for admission to the ground to liquidate the expenses.

The next day Fuller was back at King's Lynn, but this time as a member of Clarke's All-England Eleven who played on 14, 15 and 16 June another Twenty-Two of Lynn which included several members of the Lynn Club, including his brother William Pilch. The day after the game at Lynn finished the All-England team played Twenty-Two of Sleaford and District in Lincolnshire, another match unfinished because of rain with Fuller making top score of 24 out of 96 in All-England's only innings.

But it seems that Fuller had no wish to continue being employed so frequently by Clarke, and after the match at Sleaford he dropped out of the All-England side and returned to Canterbury to play in five matches for Kent.

Kent's first match of the season was at Lord's on 5, 6 and 7 July against an England team selected as usual by MCC, although it included Clarke who took ten wickets in the match and helped England to a seven-wicket victory. The next day Kent were at The Oval to play Surrey on 8, 9 and 10 July and won by six runs. The result could have been very different. According to *Scores and Biographies*, 'it was arranged by the proprietor of the ground (W.Houghton) that Martingell and Felix, though Surrey born, should form part of the Kent Eleven, to make the match more equal. They had before many times played for Kent against England and Sussex; but at cricket birth counts before residence.' Felix top-scored in the match with 70 in Kent's second innings and Martingell took eleven wickets, bowling 286 balls while the other 325 balls in the two Surrey innings were shared by three other bowlers, with Hillyer 81 balls, Willsher 92 and Mynn 152. Fuller's batting contribution was one and nought and he had to be substituted on the last day of the match near the end of Surrey's second innings due to illness.

Kent's next fixture was at Hove against Sussex on 22, 23 and 24 July. *Scores and Biographies* reported that 'F.Pilch (owing to illness) was unable to appear in this match, being the first time he has not assisted Kent since he began to play for them in 1836.' He did not play again for nearly three weeks but had recovered in time to play in the Kent v Sussex match at Tunbridge Wells at the end of July, but managed to score only ten and one and Sussex won by 53 runs. Then it was time for Canterbury Cricket Week where Kent lost against England by an innings and 2 runs. Fuller seemed to be coming back into his old form with the next highest score to Willsher's 30 in Kent's first innings, 26 out of 112, but he was caught by Parr off Grundy for nought in the second innings.

Now would be the time when Fuller, as in the previous years, would rejoin Clarke's All-England team wherever their next game was scheduled, and then spend the rest of the season touring the country. He had no personal problem with Clarke and they had just played against each other at Canterbury, so they would have been able to discuss the dates and places that Clarke had arranged. Perhaps the travelling and effort involved – he was now 48 – seemed too much for him. The convenience of the railway meant that Clarke would rush the team off the ground at the end of one match, bundle them onto a train and often have them playing somewhere else two days later, and sometimes even the following day. Their arrival at their destination would often be celebrated by large crowds followed by receptions, banquets, gala fetes and firework displays, before and during the matches and Clarke expected the players to respond with enthusiasm. Not exactly Fuller's scene perhaps. He had been playing cricket for 25 years in big matches before large crowds and had always been able to merge into the background and concentrate on the cricket while others enjoyed the limelight, letting his batting and bowling speak for him. But, for whatever reason, Fuller decided to remain in Canterbury. It proved to be a wise decision because he was able to avoid becoming involved in the start of a bitter dispute between Clarke and Wisden.

Clarke had continued to organise his fixtures very carefully and was obviously still nervous of upsetting the powers at Lord's, unaware that he should also have been more careful to avoid upsetting his contracted players. He had recruited a few outstanding younger cricketers to replace some ageing stars over the previous two years but, in common with some of the regulars, they soon had problems with his 'gangmaster' method of management and tight-fisted control of finances. One of the dissatisfied group was John Wisden, who had appeared 30 times for Clarke in 1851 but had not made himself available when All-England resumed their travels in 1852. He played in two matches which featured Clarke and most of his players, and in the Gentlemen v Players match at Lord's on 19, 20 and 21 July he was the only member of the Players team who was not currently employed by Clarke. When the All-England Eleven reached Northampton on 12 August they found him playing against them as one of the Twenty-Two of Northamptonshire. Two days later Wisden was at Canterbury playing for England against Kent alongside Clarke, who still had no suspicions of Wisden's impending treachery.

Wisden had canvassed enough players, nearly all of whom had played for Clarke in the past, to form a breakaway group which he called the United All-England Eleven, and a week later they were playing their first game at Portsmouth on 26, 27 and 28 August, while the All-England Eleven were playing at Hereford on the same days. Wisden's next fixture was at Newmarket on 30 and 31 August and 1 September, where Clarke turned up to confront Wisden and demand that he abandon his plans to continue with an independent touring team in competition with his All-England Eleven. Wisden refused to back down and called the fourteen members of his United All-England Eleven to a meeting at the Adelphi Hotel in Sheffield, on 7 September, the second day of their match against a local fifteen. Here, according to *Scores and Biographies*, they 'unanimously resolved ... that neither the members of the ... Eleven shall at any time play in any match of cricket, for or against, wherein William Clarke may have the management or control (county matches excepted) in consequence of the treatment they have received from him at Newmarket and elsewhere.'

Both groups went on to complete their remaining schedule of fixtures in September. Any hopes that Fuller Pilch would go on the road again for either Clarke or Wisden in the future were dashed when he eventually found himself drawn unwillingly into the argument near the end of the year. A letter appeared in *Bell's Life* under the signature of 'A lover of cricket' which criticised Clarke's management of the All-England Eleven and the unfair distribution of its earnings. The writer accused Clarke of retaining total control despite inviting some of his players to form a management committee, and that Fuller Pilch had refused to serve on that committee and told someone that his reasons were 'not exactly understanding how affairs were managed.' More letters followed and in due course a response from Clarke arrived 'to expose the malicious fabrications.' Clarke insisted that his players were satisfied with his methods of payment. He denied any rift with Fuller Pilch and included a statement from him: 'I am not aware of ever drawing my name from your committee, and I am very sure I never told anyone so.' Apparently, Fuller had not seen any of the correspondence in *Bell's Life* until Clarke had written to him with the details, and declared that he 'had not read the long, sickly, childish prattle.'

Putting all this unpleasantness behind him, Fuller was back at Oxford in the spring of 1853, and he was joined by Caffyn, Willsher, Grundy, Hinkley and Buttress to coach the undergraduates. They were each paid one pound a week and one shilling and sixpence for each hour of coaching. It seems that the University were determined to build a strong team ready for their annual encounter with Cambridge at Lord's in June and prepared the Magdalen ground at Cowley Common for three practice matches in twelve days. They started on 2, 3 and 4 May with a six-wicket victory over a side titled 'Eleven Players Engaged at Oxford as Bowlers', a team which included Fuller, and then beat Oxfordshire on 5 and 6 May and Oxford Harlequins on 12 and 13 May. A week later, at the Christ Church ground, Fuller brought his own England eleven again to lose to a fifteen of Oxfordshire which included most of the regular undergraduates. His work done, Fuller returned to Canterbury where he learned of his protégés' victory by an innings in the Varsity match at Lord's in mid-June.

He only played once at Lord's himself in 1853, scoring nought and twelve for Kent against England on 27 and 28 June, but appeared at the Kennington Oval in three matches. The first of these fixtures was a North v South match on 7 and 8 July scoring eight and six: both teams in this match were put together by Clarke from a selection of his All-England players.

There is no record that Fuller made any appearances for the East Kent Club that summer, but he turned out for his old friend and Kent team-mate Edward Wenman in both Benenden matches with Hollingbourne, the first in the second week of July at Benenden where his top score of 18 out of 78 helped the home team to a ten-wicket victory. Then he was persuaded by Clarke to appear in one more game for him, this time for a combined Kent and Sussex eleven against an England Eleven at Tunbridge Wells on 21, 22 and 23 July where both sides were selected by Clarke from his All-England players. This was followed by the return match between Benenden and Hollingbourne on 25 and 26 July, which was unfinished with Fuller not out in Benenden's second innings at 46 for seven, chasing 119 to win.

Fuller did not play again until Canterbury Week when Kent faced England on 15, 16 and 17 August. Five batsmen were run out in Kent's first innings, including Fuller for ten in a total of 47, and England went on to win by an innings and 179 runs. The Kent batsmen who were not run out, all lost their wickets to Clarke, seven, and Wisden, eight, who had apparently settled their differences and shared all the bowling for the England eleven. The side included players from both the All-England and United England camps.

The next week Fuller was back at The Oval in a benefit match for the old Surrey umpire Thomas Mortlock between eighteen Gentlemen of the Surrey Club and an eleven of Players on 25, 26 and 27 August. Fuller top-scored with 27 out of the Players' first innings of 86 but was absent ill from the second innings and the Gentlemen won by an innings. He made a quick recovery and was back in the Kent team for the match with Surrey at The Oval on 29, 30 and 31 August; he scored one and nought in what would be his last appearance of the season.

Fuller celebrated his fiftieth birthday before the start of the 1854 season and this milestone may have convinced him that his ability to keep playing at the highest level was coming to an end. Coaching at Oxford was apparently no longer an option, as travelling outside Kent, other than one visit to Lord's, was not attempted and even then his appearances on the field were fewer than ever before. He missed Kent's first match of the season at Hove against Sussex and the return at Gravesend.

In what proved to be farewell performances at Lord's and Canterbury he experienced the highs and the lows. For Kent against MCC at Lord's on 24 and 25 July he opened the innings and it looked like he was his old self again making top score of 32 out of 104 before being bowled by Grundy. The same bowler dismissed him again after he had made just two in the second innings. In the Cricket Week at Canterbury the Kent team had to be strengthened with four given men, Bickley, Clarke, Parr and Wisden, if they were to give the England eleven any sort of a game on 14, 15 and 16 August.[17] Although completed in two days, it was a high-scoring match – 435 four-ball overs, the equivalent of 290 six-ball overs, were sent down – won by England and Fuller's contribution was disappointing. Going in further down the order he was run out for ten in the first innings, those long legs of his finally unable to carry him quickly enough between the wickets. He was stumped off Grundy without scoring in the second innings, those same legs taking him out of his crease and then moving too slowly to bring them back to safety. This was his last match now recognised as first-class.

Fuller was persuaded by his old friend Alfred Mynn to join him at Hollingbourne to play against West Wickham on 28 and 29 August, where bad weather prevented him from having a second innings and a chance to improve on his four runs in the first. He played his very last match for Kent at Tunbridge Wells on 14, 15 and 16 September against Eighteen of Tunbridge Wells and District where proof of Kent's decline as a team to be feared was clearly demonstrated when they lost by an innings and 35 runs. Fuller made six in the first innings and was bowled by Luck for a duck in the second.

There were just a couple of club appearances in 1855 while Fuller considered his future and then he finally called time on his illustrious career. Both games were in late August for the Beverley Club against old rivals Penshurst. In the first Fuller top-scored with 17 out of 56 in the first innings, but it was only a matter of time before Penshurst ran out winners by eight wickets. In the return at Canterbury, on 30 and 31 August, he managed only six runs in the first innings and in a determined attempt to turn the clock back, he decided to have a bowl when it was Penshurst's turn to bat. He took three wickets and helped restrict the lead to only eight runs. It appears that this extra physical effort was the final nail in the coffin of his cricket career, as the scorecard shows that he was 'absent' from Beverley's second innings. He never played again.

His business with Edward Martin came to an end at about this time, with the publication of a notice in the *London Gazette* above the names of Fuller Pilch and Edward Martin reading: 'Notice is hereby given that the partnership heretofore existing between us the undersigned, Fuller Pilch and Edward Martin, in the business of Cricket Bat Makers at Oxford, under

---

17   Kent thus fielded three players over 50: Clarke was 55, Wenman and Pilch were 50. Perhaps it was this match he was referring to when he suggested to Fred Gale many years later that perhaps he and his colleagues played on too long. There have been only five instances of first-class sides having three players over 50. Three were before 1854. The only instance since was the MCC side which played Cambridge University at Fenner's in 1953, with G.O.B.Allen, J.M.Sims and R.E.S Wyatt on board. MCC won.

the firm of Pilch and Martin, is this day dissolved by mutual consent. Witness our hands this 2nd day of November 1855.'

Chapter Twenty-Four
Umpire, coach, groundsman, bat-maker and mine host

Fuller remained groundsman at the St Lawrence Ground for which he received £20 a year, but without the regular payments coming in from match appearances, apart from occasional engagements to stand as umpire at only £1 a match and irregular requests for the manufacture of cricket bats and other accessories,[18] he needed to find some new employment to provide a steady income. He was still in partnership with nephew William as tailors in Canterbury but there may not have been enough custom for them to work together full-time, even if Fuller did have more time available. They considered the options very carefully and came up with the perfect solution. Although Fuller had many years experience as landlord of an inn or tavern, taking on such a responsibility again on his own at his age might have been too much for him. But if William joined him to share the workload they would be taking over an established business with a clientele of regular customers which could be increased by exploiting Fuller's celebrity status while he continued to make and supply cricket equipment. There was the added advantage of free accommodation for Hephzibah and little Alfred as well, and when the opportunity came to move into the Saracen's Head on Burgate Street, near the centre of Canterbury, just outside the city wall, they didn't hesitate. The exact date of their move is not clear but an announcement appeared in a Canterbury Business Directory for 1855:

F. & W.PILCH (Successors to J.E.Bassenden)
SARACEN'S HEAD INN, 73 Burgate Street, Canterbury.
F. and W. P. respectfully inform their Friends and the Public generally, that they have taken the above OLD ESTABLISHED INN, where it will be their duty to accommodate their friends, and all who may honour them with a visit, in a manner that shall ensure their comfort and satisfaction.
Genuine Superior Liquors of all kinds, choice old Wines, Scotch ales, bottled Porter, etc, etc. Excellent well-aired beds. Capital Stall Stabling and Coach House.
N.B. Cricket Bats, Balls, Leggings, and every requisite for Cricketing

---

18 The development of the cane-handled bat, turned using machinery, by Thomas Nixon in 1853, ensured that bat-making became a largely 'workshop' activity carried out by several men working together. This gradually brought to an end the business of individual bat-makers working at home which Fuller had sometimes practised in the past. Later on the trade became even more specialised and 'workshop-bound' when makers started to insert strips of rubber or whalebone into handles to reduce jarring.

The change of employment and accommodation must have suited them all, as the 1861 census tells us that they were still in residence after six years. William is listed as 'innkeeper', with Fuller using the all-embracing title of 'cricketer' this time. They have a resident cook, barmaid, housemaid, 'boots' and an ostler for the stables. There are two boarders, one is a seventeen-year-old jockey, and the other has put himself down as a horse-dealer.

After his retirement in 1855 Fuller was not completely lost to cricket, of course. There was still work to do at St Lawrence's as groundsman, coaching at King's School, and he stood as umpire during Canterbury Cricket Week in one or both matches every year from 1855 to 1866. Other occasional umpire duties in Kent took him to Tunbridge Wells, Maidstone, Chatham, Cranbrook and Folkestone, as well as trips outside the county to Hove, Kennington Oval and Lord's.[19] He was asked to play in a benefit match for William Hillyer in 1858, but did not feel up to joining the eighteen 'Veterans', including Thomas Adams, William Martingell, Thomas Box, Alfred Mynn and Ned Wenman, who faced an England eleven at The Oval. He was not involved in the formation of a New Kent County Cricket Club at Maidstone in 1859 either. The club, with Ned Wenman and Alfred Mynn on the committee, would represent the county as a whole with matches to be shared among several grounds, leaving William de Chair Baker with sole responsibility for the Canterbury Cricket Week. Fuller's loyalties naturally stayed with Canterbury, although he continued to travel to the other grounds to act as umpire for county matches when requested.

The face of fortitude. Fuller Pilch in a studio photograph taken in 1861, aged 57. Rowland Bowen, writing in 1970, thought he had an 'air about him of Abraham Lincoln'. Lincoln was United States President from 1861 to 1865; Fuller lacked his loquacity, but outlived him.

---

19   He stood in 29 first-class matches between 1855 and 1866. Other games may come to light in the future.

When Alfred Mynn died in 1861, Fuller, together with Ned Wenman, Edgar Willsher, William de Chair Baker, W.South Norton and Edward Bligh, was asked to serve on a committee that was set up to establish a testimonial fund for him. A portion of the contributions was set aside for the erection of a tombstone at Thurnham churchyard, and the committee resolved that the remainder be invested and the interest used to support the maintenance of a retired Kent cricketer to be chosen each year.

Fuller made at least two appearances as umpire in 1862 where the context and location are surprising. Fuller had severed all connection with the All-England Eleven nine years earlier and had not travelled further north than Lord's in St. John's Wood since he stopped playing, when out of the blue he was recorded as standing as umpire at Barnsley on 26 May for the match between Twenty of Yorkshire and the All-England Eleven, followed by a first-class match at Sheffield, where Yorkshire entertained Kent. This short tour had started at Sheffield one week earlier when they played Twenty-Two of the Sheffield Yorkshire Club, and although the names of the umpires were not recorded, it seems very likely that Fuller would have been travelling with the team from the start and had stood in that match as well. But why did he suddenly break his settled routine in the south and spend three weeks in Yorkshire? It couldn't have been the money – his fee for umpiring would have barely covered his expenses – so there had to be a good reason to abandon his comfort zone and head off north. The answer, I believe, can be found in the census listing for 1861, almost twelve months earlier. Fuller's brother William had moved with his family from the Royal Oak Inn at King's Lynn to the King William tavern in the centre of Sheffield, and is registered as 'publican' and 'bat-maker'. So Fuller, hearing of the All-England Eleven tour, had added himself to the party to take advantage of the venues and pay one of his family a visit. A reunion of brothers after ten years, both realising, perhaps, that there might not be many more opportunities.

Fuller was back at Chatham a week later, umpiring the Kent match with Cambridgeshire and when it was time for Canterbury Cricket Week he stood as umpire in a match full of controversy involving the Grace family. Doctor Henry Grace and his wife Martha, parents of the brothers W.G., E.M., and G.F., had been regular visitors to Canterbury for the Cricket Week in previous years. In August 1862, Dr. Grace heard that both the England and MCC teams were short of players, so he sent a telegram to his eldest son, E.M., instructing him to drop everything and get to Canterbury as fast as possible. He arrived in time to turn out for England against Fourteen of Kent and his 56 was the second-highest score in the match. He was then asked to play for MCC, although he was not a member, in the all-amateur match between Twelve Gentlemen of Kent and the Twelve Gentlemen of MCC. When the Kent captain, W.South Norton, learnt of the selection, he protested against E.M.'s eleventh-hour inclusion, and a compromise may have been suggested that the teams be reduced to eleven a side. The MCC captain, R.A.Fitzgerald, refused to back down and an impasse was reached until William de Chair Baker, who still had sole responsibility for organising the week, intervened and ordered the game to proceed, with E.M.Grace playing for MCC. It is not known whether Fuller was involved in settling this pre-match dispute but his presence must have had a calming effect upon the situation. Even so, Kent took the field 'under protest' when the game started.

To rub salt in Kent's wounds, E.M. took five of their first-innings wickets and then scored an unbeaten 192, the highest-ever score seen at the St Lawrence ground. He then took ten wickets in Kent's second innings. It might have been all eleven wickets if one of the Kent Gentlemen, R.J.Streatfeild, had not been absent. Kent's captain, W.South Norton, who came from the Town Malling Club, never played at Canterbury again, either by choice or because he was no longer welcome.

There was another young son in the Grace family who was showing promise as a cricketer, but Fuller only ever stood as umpire in one match at Canterbury in which W.G. played. In 1866, the Gentlemen of the South played the 'wandering' amateur side I Zingari and Fuller watched the young man, destined to dominate the game for the next thirty years, score 30 and 50 in his two innings for the Gentlemen. There is no record of any conversation between the two great players. W.G. never mentioned meeting Fuller Pilch in any of his memoirs, and W.G. does not appear in any of Fuller's conversations with Frederick Gale. The game had moved on, over-arm bowling was now permitted, wickets were better prepared and the age gap between a 62-year-old legend of the game and an earnest 18-year-old may have been impossible to bridge with attempts by either to discuss batting skills and techniques. Fuller did tell Gale in 1869 that 'Daft, Jupp and Mr Grace were three of the most extraordinary players he ever saw in his life,' but the Mr Grace he referred to was E.M., not W.G.

Much altered after Fuller's time, the Saracen's Head Inn, dating from the seventeenth century, was demolished in 1969 to make way for the Canterbury inner ring road. This picture shows the building shortly before its destruction.

Chapter Twenty-Five
A pipe in Fuller Pilch's back parlour

Whenever the author and journalist Frederick Gale had the opportunity, he would return to Canterbury to enjoy a week-end break, or what he called being 'out on a run from Saturday till Monday', and he would always pay his friend Fuller Pilch a visit at the Saracen's Head on the Sunday evening. Gale described his routine as 'cathedral in the morning, luncheon etc; in the afternoon, tea, claret cup, etc., in the garden under the trees near the cathedral; and in the evening, a quiet talk in Fuller's private room passed the day.' He would make notes of Fuller's opinions on various cricket subjects and in 1887 collated them together as a chapter in his book *The Game of Cricket* as if they came from one long conversation while sharing 'a pipe in Fuller Pilch's back parlour'. Most of the chapter consists of Fuller's rambling assessments of players, in no particular order, in reply to Gale's request: 'Now, Pilch, let's have a talk about the old Kent eleven' and I have extracted and re-assembled them under various headings, accompanied by their Kent statistical records between 1825 and 1859. Perhaps we should imagine his remarks made in a gentle Norfolk accent.

Fuller prefaced his reminiscences with an evaluation of the team as a whole: 'Now I will tell you just what the Kent eleven was to my mind: it was an eleven of brothers, who knew one another, and never knew what jealousy was.' He knew how proud they were of their county: 'I know this, that we played for the honour of the county and the love of the game first,' but he did not overlook those who had come forward with finance and support for the development of the cricket in Kent and elsewhere, 'and, of course, the gentlemen took care of us in the second place.' Before moving on to individual players, he then insisted on putting his opinions in perspective: 'I don't say that men can't play as well now as then; but I do say that a stronger band of cricketers was never got together than our eleven at its best.'

Before looking at the batsmen, bowlers, wicket-keepers, long-stops and other fieldsmen, Fuller revealed some of the pressures behind choosing new players.

Team Selection

Fuller always tried to keep a couple of places for young amateurs from the public schools or universities but insisted that:

> money couldn't get a gentleman into the Kent eleven. Some one might say to me, 'Pilch, Mr So-and-so, the rich brewer or banker's son, wants

to play in the county eleven.' 'Very well,' I used to say, 'Let me see him make a "good hands" against good bowling, and see what he is worth in the field, and if he is good enough he shall play.' I didn't much like gentlemen in the eleven unless they were heart and soul cricketers; they might be up late dining, or playing billiards or cards or what not overnight, and lose a match; but I knew a good one when I saw him.

There were three whom he especially remembered:

Mr Emilius Bayley, Mr Edward Banks, and Mr Edward Swann – the last was our long-stop very often – and they did work. Mr Bayley did not play often, but he was a fine long-leg and cover-point, and no mistake. He brought his name from Eton. Then Mr Edward Banks: I found him down Sandwich way, where his property lay. He and his youngest brother, Mr William, were the quickest between the wickets I ever did see, and Mr Edward was one of the smartest in the long-field. He was like a thoroughbred horse, for no matter how far the ball was off he would try; and when I sung out, 'Go to her, Mr Edward! Go to her!' he would outrun himself almost, and as sure as ever he got his hands to her, the ball was like a rat in a trap.

Bayley was the most successful of these four players, scoring 236 runs at 13.88 for Kent in 12 first-class matches.

Long-stop

A fielder 'condemned to hard labour' according to Fuller, as he did little more than retrieve the ball as quickly as he could in the days of uneven pitches and the ball streaking or bouncing past a wicket-keeper without gloves or pads. As playing conditions improved, Fuller recognised the long-stop's ability to stop balls rather than chase after them: 'I think long-stopping is generally better now, for the ground is rolled for long-stop, and he is made one of the most important men in the field, and long-stop was looked on pretty much as a man who was condemned to hard labour; though my nephew, William Pilch, was as good as ever I saw.'

Walter Mynn was also pretty good in that position, and Fuller remembered that when his brother Alfred first arrived, 'ne'er a man in England but his brother Walter would long-stop for him' and Ned Wenman, as wicket-keeper, 'didn't stop every ball, or every other ball, perhaps, for he left his long-stop to do his own work. "What's the good of Mr Walter Mynn for long-stop," he used to say, "if I am to do all his work and knock my hands to pieces? No; let him do his work, and I will do mine."'

Wicket-keeping

When it came to the real work of a wicket-keeper, Fuller was certain he had played with the best one of all: 'Just think of Ned Wenman behind the wicket: was there ever a better?' Fuller recalled his expertise at stumping batsmen out: 'I can see Ned Wenman now with his eye on the batsman's foot and the crease, without any pads or gloves; and sure as a man showed a sign of drawing his foot, he took the ball close to the bails and just broke the wicket, and looked at the umpire if he thought it was out; and it was very seldom that e'er an umpire said "No" to him, for he was a real good judge.' In 61 first-class matches for Kent, Wenman took 54 catches and made 33 stumpings.

Fielding

Fuller expected fieldsmen to be alert to opportunities: 'A good many gentlemen, and players too, are afraid of dropping a catch, and they drop back for the first bound, instead of going to her neck or nothing. Nothing pleases the public so much as a hard running catch, or does a man more credit, and every catch ought to be TRIED if possible.' He rated several Kent players as top-class fieldsmen: 'Dorrinton, what a useful man he was! Well balanced everywhere, a fine field. Tom Adams in the long-field, and Mr Felix point. There was a pair for you! How often did you ever see Tom Adams miss a catch, or miss throwing a wicket down, if Mr Felix called to him to throw in the chance of throwing a man out? And how often did you see Mr Felix allow an overthrow if he called on Adams to take a shot? Why, never, and that's about it.' Closer to the wicket, he thought 'there never was a better short-slip than Hillyer, or than Alfred Mynn,' and Fuller could not resist including himself: 'I suppose Fuller Pilch weren't much of a dunce at mid-off, and not a very bad judge of the game.' Fuller himself took 45 catches in his 84 first-class games for Kent, but Tom Adams, with 78 in 99 matches, and William Hillyer, with 73 in 82, were numerically more successful.

Bowling

Fuller had a list of the best bowlers in the Kent eleven: 'Alfred Mynn and Hillyer, with Tom Adams, Martingell, Hinkley, Mr Frederick Fagge for a change, and Edgar Willsher somewhat later. Very often we didn't want the change, if the ground was strong enough to bear Alfred Mynn; for if the ground was rotten, he dug a grave with his left foot.' He added: 'Ground and weather didn't matter to Hillyer; rough or smooth, wet or dry, sand or mud, he could put a ball on a sixpence, and he did just what Ned Wenman told him. You remember, when the ground was a little hard how Alfred would drop her short, and the ball would cut right across from the on to the off, and hum like a top.'

Fuller remembered that there were also occasions when he and Alfred Mynn were on opposite teams so he could speak from experience about his bowling: 'I never liked playing against Alfred Mynn, for he and I were like brother in the first place; and in the second, he would drop 'em short and put all the steam on if the ground was hard, for he knew my play.' He went on: 'And people mayn't think it, but a short-pitched ball, cutting right across from the on to the off, is about the nastiest stuff you can have; for if she shoots she wants a deal of play to stop her, and if she jumps up "knuckle high", it is a job to keep her away from short-slip, or from popping up.' They actually faced each other in 65 matches and Mynn captured Fuller's wicket 34 times out of 111 innings. For Kent, William Hillyer, with 497 recorded wickets in 82 matches, and Alfred Mynn, with 417 in ninety games, were the most successful of Fuller's bowling contemporaries with the county.

I have not included the record of Edgar Willsher as he continued to play for another five years after Fuller Pilch had passed on, and ended his Kent career with 786 wickets from 145 matches. Fuller did have a good look at his bowling as they played together in 12 matches before Fuller's retirement, during which Willsher took 39 wickets. Fuller appears to have been confused when he named Frederick Fagge in his list of the best Kent bowlers. Fagge had rarely bowled in any of his 14 county matches and only taken only one wicket, although he had taken 85 wickets when playing for the 'Gentlemen of Kent' in 23 matches between 1833 and 1853. But Fuller had enjoyed a closer look at Fagge's bowling when they appeared together in six matches for Norfolk between 1844 and 1847 during which Fagge had taken 18 wickets and this would seem to have been the basis for Fuller's assessment.

Batting

Naturally, Fuller had plenty to say about the Kent batting:

> When we came to our batting, we managed to all work together somehow. Ned Wenman played back and cut, and I was about the most forward player in England; and between us we puzzled the bowlers sometimes. My play, as you know, was a good deal what they called 'Pilch's poke', because I relied on smothering the ball and drove her forward. Mr Walter Mynn and Hillyer were two useful ones, though neither of them batted in any style, and Walter was very stiff. But those two never knew fear, and if we were likely to want a few notches at the finish, I always kept them back to the last; or if we had a quarter of an hour to time I would put them in and say, 'You two bide till the clock strikes seven, and don't think of the notches.' Ay, and many a time they've done it too!

There was one batsman Fuller praised above all:

> Mr Felix on his own day was my man. He was not so safe as Mr Charles Taylor of Sussex, or Joseph Guy of Nottingham, or Ned Wenman, or perhaps me; but when he got to work, and the ground and the light suited him, it was a wonderful sight to see him bat. He knew the whole science of the game, and had a hand and eye such as no one e'er beat him at; and when he saw the ball was pretty well safe to keep outside the off-stump, it was a beautiful thing to see him throw his right foot forward - for, as you remember, he was left-handed - and do a little bit

of tiptoe-ing, with his bat over his shoulder; and if he did get the ball full, and it missed the watches, you heard her hit the palings on the off-side almost as soon as she left his bat. And what a temper Mr Felix had! And what a laugh too! And didn't he like to go on with old Lillywhite a bit! He used to have a little joke when he came in. He would go into the middle, and pick up a little bit of paper or straw, or what not, and look up to old Lillywhite, who was a little impatient, waiting with the ball in his hand. 'Good-morning, Mr Lillywhite! Halloa! A cricket-match on to-day, eh? And you a-bowling? Well, let's have an innings.' Well, old Lillywhite would be a little bit cross perhaps, sometimes, and would answer him a little sharp, and 'You go and mind your batting, MUSTER Felix, and I will mind my bowling,' and it was wonderful to see the care Mr Felix took for an over or two. It was no use sending him up one to hit with an England or Sussex field round until Mr Felix felt 'set'; but directly he knew that hand and eye were master, to it he went, and if he got the chance he DID punish the bowling.

Fuller had special memories of one other batsman: 'Tom Adams, too, was a real good one in a match. He was never a first-rate bat, or a first-rate bowler, but a magnificent field, and he worked like a horse, and if the bowling got a little loose he was a rare punisher. He was a curious customer, and looked so knowing, with a corkscrew "gypsy curl" on each side of his face. And couldn't he throw, and shoot, or play skittles, or anything else! And though he wasn't a quarrelsome man, if there was a row and he was insulted, he was ready for any number – one down, t'other come on.'

Fuller doesn't include Alfred Mynn in his list of batsmen, probably because he saw him predominately as a match-winning bowler. Mynn often batted for Kent lower down the order after an extensive bowling session, or Ned Wenman and Fuller were saving him for one to come. When Mynn joined the 'Gentlemen of Kent' or played for the Gentlemen against the Players at Lord's, his reputation dictated that he must go in early, and this is reflected in his record for both teams, 1,402 runs in 50 matches with an average of 15.40, whereas in 90 matches for Kent he averaged only 12.71. Fuller himself was easily the most successful of the Kent batsmen of his time, scoring 2,844 runs at 19.61 for the county in 84 first-class matches. The other players scoring a thousand runs or more were Tom Adams with 2,291 runs, average 12.58 in 99 matches; Nicholas Felix with 1,528 runs, average 16.79 in 52 matches; and Ned Wenman with 1,063 runs, average 10.42 in 61 matches. Fuller was dismissed caught in 40 per cent of his completed innings in first-class cricket, three or four percentage points less often than these contemporaries, perhaps a consequence of his ability to play forward and 'get over' the ball.

It is clear from Gale's reporting of his conversations with Fuller Pilch that our subject understood the affection and admiration which were felt for the Kent elevens of the 1830s and 1840s. This esteem is nowadays most apparent in the well-known verses by W.J.Prowse published in 1861 by

Bell's Life at the time of Alfred Mynn's death and noted in this book as an ilustration on page 56. In reporting that every man of the eleven was 'glad and proud to play his part', and in listing the five main players – Felix, Wenman, Hillyer, Fuller Pilch and Alfred Mynn – those verses seem to accord with Fuller's own modest view, from the tone of his remarks to Gale, that Kent's successes were attributable to the combined skills of a group of players rather than to particular individual performances.

When Gale asked what he thought of present cricket, Fuller was surprisingly unimpressed, bearing in mind that, to future historians, cricket was in the process of entering a golden age: 'There's too much of it, and you know what a man is going to do before he does it. It is like seeing a play over and over again, when they come in at the same place and go out at the same place every night; there is more business than pleasure in it, too often.' Some of his other opinions sound familiar to the twenty-first century lover of cricket: 'There is so much swagger and dress in the cricket-field now sometimes, and so much writing and squabbling with committees and secretaries and players about cricket, that I often feel that the heart of the game is going, and that very many are playing for their own glory more than for their county now.'

Chapter Twenty-Six
A pension and a monument

By 1867 Fuller's health was deteriorating. He was no longer able to take an active role in the management of the Saracen's Head Inn where his nephew William, as the licensed victualler, was running into financial difficulties, although he continued trading under their old 'style' as F. & W.Pilch. Fuller had been retained as groundsman at the St Lawrence Ground, but even that was now beyond him. The *Kent Herald* later reported that during the years 1867 and 1868 he was much affected by rheumatism and much of his work had to be done for him. It added:

> During the summer of 1868 a movement was made for a subscription to be entered into to give him a maintenance, but although it was taken in hand by several gentlemen, little result was made until in the Cricket Week some £40 was collected on the ground, and the Old Stagers added £10 from their fund. In the expectation that this subscription would be equalled by gifts from other friends in the ensuing year, one pound per week was paid to the veteran, which, with his frugal requirements, kept him in comfort; although the renewed subscriptions last year fell very short, and the fund therefore became entirely exhausted this spring. A few gentlemen guaranteed to co-operate with the Hon Secretary of the Beverley Club, and the stipend was accordingly kept up until his death.

The award of a pension was agreed only just in time. In 1868 William had been arrested for debts of £698[20] and taken to Maidstone Gaol, but was released on 22 May 1869. The fall-out from the collapse of the Overend, Gurney bank in 1866, with liabilities of £11 million, had caused something of a panic in London, Liverpool, Manchester, Norwich, Derby and Bristol, and triggered off a business downturn similar to the financial crisis of 2007. There was a minor recession between 1867 and 1869 and businesses everywhere were feeling the effects of the tightening of commercial credit, with many bankruptcies in the wine and beer trade.[21] A local factor referred to in William's bankruptcy hearings was that farmers and butchers had previously put up overnight at the Saracen's Head, but now travelled back and forth on the new London, Chatham, and Dover Railway which had opened in 1861. It was William's bad luck that the new bankruptcy laws introduced in 1869, thanks largely to the campaign of Charles Dickens and the success of his novel 'Little Dorrit' in drawing attention to the iniquities of imprisonment for debt, came too late to save him from prison.

---

20   About £32,000 at 2010 prices.
21   In the week of William's bankruptcy, the courts dealt with another 45 cases in the licensed trade.

An announcement eventually appeared in the *London Gazette* of 15 June 1869:

> William Pilch, late of the Saracen's Head Inn, Burgate Street, Canterbury, Kent, licensed victualler, having been adjudged bankrupt by a Registrar attending at Maidstone Gaol, on the 19th day of May, 1869, and the adjudication being directed to be prosecuted at the Court of Bankruptcy, London aforesaid, a public sitting, for the said bankrupt to pass his Last Examination, and make application for his Discharge, will be held before Edward Holroyd, Esq., a Commissioner of the said Court, on the 9th day of July next, at the said Court, at Basinghall-street, in City of London, at two o'clock in the afternoon precisely, the day last aforesaid being the day limited for the said bankruptcy to surrender. Mr Peter Paget of 22 Basinghall-street, London, is the official Assignee, and Mr Hicklin, of Swan Street, Trinity Square, is the solicitor acting in the Bankruptcy.

William evidently reached an understanding with his creditors and his petition for bankruptcy was granted, with his principal creditor being William Rideal, a wine merchant of Union Street, Southwark. He left the court to return to Canterbury and rejoin Fuller, Hephzibah and Alfred at 5 Lower Bridge Street. Frederick Gale wrote: 'The last time I saw Fuller Pilch was a few months before his bankruptcy, which, I believe, killed him. The world did not prosper with him as it ought, and he was out of spirits, and got so excited about the old times that I had to drop the subject.' It is not clear whether Gale had his facts wrong and believed that Fuller had indeed been made bankrupt himself, or whether he was describing Fuller's natural distress at the prospect of William's financial ruin which was, to all intents and purposes, his own. Whatever the case, it seems that Gale was right about one thing, Fuller had less than a year to live.

Fuller Pilch passed away on Sunday, 1 May 1870, at Lower Bridge Street. The *Herald* reported: 'Poor old Fuller's gone! After an illness of about a fortnight, he died peacefully and without pain on Sunday afternoon last, attended in his last moments by his nephew and other members of his family.' The paper also gave some clues that go some way to explain the reasons for his financial decline in the final years of his life: 'it would indeed be a sour and mean disposition which could prompt ill-speaking of poor old Fuller now he's gone. He certainly was not a shrewd businessman, but he was kindly, unselfish, and essentially manly – ready to help in his way anyone needing help, never giving offence, loath to take offence, but never permitting offence without rebuke.'

Whatever the circumstances, the news of Fuller's death came as a shock to the residents of Canterbury and the rest of Kent. The *Kentish Gazette* printed an obituary notice which reviewed his career at Bury, Norwich, Town Malling and Canterbury, and confirmed that he had been 'failing for some months' but the immediate cause of his death was 'dropsy', an accumulation of fluid around the heart, which doctors would today record as congestive heart failure.

Bridge Street, Canterbury in 2010.
Fuller Pilch lived in this corner of the city at the time of his death.

The funeral took place on Thursday, 5 May. The *Kentish Gazette* told its readers:

> The remains of Fuller Pilch, the once famous cricketer, whose death was announced in last Tuesday's Gazette, were interred in St. Gregory's Cemetery, on Thursday afternoon. Deference to the wish of the deceased, which if not actually expressed, was most certainly implied by his reserved manners, prevented any organised arrangement for his numerous friends to follow the much-respected cricket champion to his last resting-place; but this, however, did not prevent about forty gentlemen citizens of Canterbury who had for many years been in the habit of meeting and enjoying the society of 'old Fuller' from assembling in Lower Bridge Street, and following in procession the funeral cortege from thence to the cemetery. In the burial-ground a large party of persons, assembled to pay a last token of respect to a man second to none as a cricketer, and certainly unequalled in those qualities which command universal esteem and regard. A suggestion has, we understand, been made that some permanent record of Fuller Pilch's qualities, professional and private, should be made, and if this intention be carried out, we are assured the necessary funds to accomplish it will be speedily forthcoming.

By a strange coincidence, in the same edition of the newspaper and only a few inches below the report of the funeral, an advance notice gives details of a lecture, 'The Story of Cricket', to be given by Frederick Gale in Canterbury a few days later. The *Gazette* reported: 'It is to be illustrated by a cartoon of a match played in 1743, together with drawings of bats from

1740 to the present time. It will be divided into two parts, the first relating to the Origins of Cricket - rise and progress of the Old Hambledon, Star and Garter, White Conduit and Marylebone Clubs, the days of Underhand Bowling; and the second to the Rise of Round Arm Bowling - the great days of the old Kent Eleven - the Average System.' The newspaper added: 'In a city and county so noted for a love of and proficiency in the "noble and manly game", we surely need urge nothing in recommendation of such a theme to the attention of our readers.'

The idea of a memorial to Fuller Pilch would no doubt have been raised during Gale's lecture and one day later, another notice appeared confirming that 'a fund is being raised for the purpose of erecting some suitable memorial to the late Fuller Pilch, whose fame as a cricketer needs no word of ours to enhance. But beyond his marvellous skill as a cricketer, he bore throughout his career an unimpeachable character as a man.' The *Gazette* added: 'All our sporting contemporaries have borne honourable testimony to his integrity. He was before the public ... from early youth to old age, and bore a spotless character throughout.' The newspaper asked that contributions be sent to the secretary of the Pilch Memorial Fund Committee. Details of a meeting of the committee appeared on another page: 'At a meeting of the Friends of the late Fuller Pilch (well-known for many years in Kent and throughout the Kingdom as an unrivalled cricketer) held at the Fleece Hotel, Canterbury, on Monday evening, 9th May, it was resolved that, it being desirable that some suitable memorial should be erected over his grave in St Gregory's burying ground, as a mark of the esteem in which he was held as a man and a Christian.' The meeting decided that subscriptions should be solicited for that purpose, and that they be limited to five shillings from each subscriber.

Contributions to the fund flooded in and during 1871 a memorial was erected over his grave consisting of a massive square pedestal and obelisk twelve feet high.[22] It bore an inscription, unfortunately with the wrong year of birth: 'Fuller Pilch, born at Horningtoft, Norfolk March 17th 1803. Died at Canterbury May 1st 1870 aged 67. This monument is erected to the memory of Fuller Pilch by upwards of 200 friends, to mark their admiration of his skill as a cricketer and his worth as a man. Viro simlici, constanti probo.' This last sentence accorded him approval as 'a straightforward man, constant and honest.'

Some years later Frederick Gale went to the churchyard and was less than impressed:

> I paid a visit a year or two back to his grave to see his monument and the bas-relief of him retiring from a broken wicket. I pictured to myself his grand commanding figure, and in imagination re-peopled the old Town Malling ground with the brave old Kentish yeomen, and could

---

[22] In the meanwhile, the eighth issue of Wisden Cricketers' Almanack, for 1871, had appeared. A slim publication of just 152 pages, it was not then given to long obituary notices. Even so, it said firmly: 'Pilch was *the* great batsman of his time, and the finest forward player known.'

Fuller Pilch's memorial in St Gregory's churchyard, Canterbury as it was in the 1960s.

The new headstone in the churchyard has added to the inaccuracy of the obelisk it has replaced.

hear their ringing cheer as their favourite, in his first over, broke the ice and made one of his brilliant forward drives just out of reach of point and mid-off, and I could hear Pilch's voice, 'Come on: easy three, Mister Felix!' And I looked forward with interest to see him represented in marble; but guess my horror when I found the bas-relief to be nothing more or less than an accurate representation of a short paralytic baboon who had sprained his leg in jumping over a broken hurdle.

In 1922 the offending bas-relief was replaced by a bronze plaque showing Fuller at the wicket after a famous lithograph by the artist G.F.Watts. When the churchyard became redundant in 1978 the pedestal was taken to the Kent County Cricket headquarters at the St Lawrence Ground and the bronze plaque placed on the wall of the committee room.

It is encouraging to know that the importance of Fuller Pilch has not been forgotten in Norfolk either. In 2004 the two-hundredth anniversary of the year of his birth was celebrated by the Horningtoft Heritage Society with a festival cricket match played in nineteenth-century costume during the village's summer fête and an exhibition of the Pilch family history was assembled for display in the village church by cricket historian Terry Taylor, author of 'Fuller Pilch: The Champion of Bury St Edmunds' in *Cricket Lore* magazine.

The festival match played at Horningtoft in July 2004 to celebrate the bicentenary of the birth of Fuller Pilch.

One hundred and thirty-eight years after his death, Fuller Pilch was once again the centre of attention. 'They still can't get him out as legendary batsman's grave blocks Concert Hall plan' was the headline in *The Times* of 25 June 2008. The newspaper went on to explain: 'Building work in the churchyard of St Gregory's, in Canterbury, cannot proceed until his remains, along with the remains of about 200 others, have been disinterred and reburied away from the site of the proposed music centre. The trouble is, the planners have no idea where he actually is.'

Canterbury Christ Church University, who proposed to build the 350-seater auditorium on the now redundant and unkempt graveyard, announced: 'We have been advised that Fuller Pilch is buried within the churchyard and that his memorial stone was moved. However, his name does not appear on the initial survey of the graves undertaken as part of our planning application. We cannot confirm the location of his grave until a further survey is carried out if planning permission is granted. If it is granted, all the remains affected will be reburied in a memorial garden in a corner of the churchyard.' All work ground to a halt until a relative, Peter Pilch, produced a photograph taken in the 1950s of the memorial, with his mother standing next to the grave, which could be identified as being on the south side of St Gregory's, whereas the music centre was being built on the north side. As the grave would be unaffected, a new memorial tombstone was erected. It had been intended that this would bear the same details as the original of 1870, but his birthplace is now incorrectly spelt. Further research, carried out since the erection of the new headstone, has shown that it should have been positioned above a double plot about fifteen yards away from its present position. None of this is particularly satisfactory, of course.

However, now that the churchyard's future has been determined, we can be reasonably sure that the remains of Fuller Pilch can rest at peace. Perhaps though, once the new music centre is completed, we should think of them being gently stirred on a summer's evening whenever a faint melody is carried past them on the breeze, by their recollection of the violin playing of his colleague, Nicholas Felix.

Acknowledgements

I would like to thank a number of individuals and organisations who helped my research in many ways, including tracking down and supplying copies of various newspaper reports of matches: Mick Pope, Wombwell Cricket Lovers' Society; Willie Sugg, Cambridgeshire cricket historian; Colin Munford, Suffolk County Cricket Association historian; Julian Lawton-Smith, Oxfordshire cricket historian; David Robertson, curator, Kent County Cricket Club; Pauline Chapman, Horningtoft Heritage Society; Jeanette Earl, Canterbury Christ Church University; Peter Henderson, King's School, Canterbury; Rhiannon Markless, independent researcher at the National Archives Centre; Anne Thorburn and Christopher Hall, Canterbury Library; Sheila Malloch and Ali Heaps at the Cathedral Archives, Canterbury; Craig Bowen at the Canterbury City Museum and Neil Robinson at the MCC Library at Lord's. Staff at Bromley Library, the British Library, the East Kent Archives Centre, Maidstone Reference Library and West Malling Library have been most helpful. My thanks also to Philip Bailey, Roger Moulton and Duncan McLeish who have contributed statistical and classical knowledge to the text; and Terry Taylor at Bury St Edmunds who helped me kick-start the book by providing all of the research for his article in *Cricket Lore* and details of the bi-centenary celebrations of the birth of Fuller Pilch organised by the Horningtoft Heritage Society.

I must express particular thanks to Peter Wynne-Thomas at Trent Bridge, Nottingham, who read the first draft of the text and identified inconsistencies, errors and omissions that needed to be corrected.

Special thanks are also due to David Jeater for his encouragement, suggestions and calm but firm guidance through to completion. Zahra Ridge has designed the cover; Peter Griffiths has attended to the time-consuming task of typesetting and has overseen the production process; Roger Mann, Steve Lewis and Canterbury City Museum have helped with the illustrations; Kit Bartlett and David Kelly have brought their proofreading expertise to bear. My thanks to them all.

B.R.

Bibliography

The principal publications consulted are the following:

1 Collections of scores

Haygarth, Arthur, *Frederick Lillywhite's Scores and Biographies, Volumes 1 to 15*, various publishers, various years

ACS [compilers], *Important Cricket Matches 1820–1863* (seven volumes), ACS Publications, various years

2 Newspapers and magazines

Bell's Life in London
The Bury and Norwich Post
The Cambridge Independent Press
The Kent Herald
The Kentish Gazette
The Kentish Observer
The Leicester Herald
The Leicester Journal
The Maidstone Journal
The Norfolk Chronicle
The Norwich Mercury
The Oxford Journal
Perry's Bankruptcy Weekly Gazette
The Sheffield and Rotherham Independent
The Sheffield Chronicle
The Sheffield Mercury
The Sportsman
The Suffolk Chronicle
The Times

3 Books

Altham, H.S. and E.W.Swanton, *A History of Cricket* (Fourth Edition), George Allen and Unwin, 1962

Barty-King, Hugh, *Quilt Winders and Pod Shavers*, Macdonald and Jane's, 1979

Birley, Derek, *A Social History of Cricket*, Aurum Press, 1999

Bowen, Rowland, *Cricket: A History of its Growth and Development*, Eyre and Spottiswoode, 1970

Bibliography

Brodribb, Gerald, *Felix on the Bat*, Eyre and Spottiswoode, 1962
Caffyn, William, *Seventy-One Not Out*, Blackwood and Sons, 1899
Daft, Richard, *Kings of Cricket*, Simpkin, Marshall, 1893
Davies, Peter, *From Magdalen to Merger*, University of Huddersfield, 2004
Denison, William, *Cricket: Sketches of the Players*, Simpkin, Marshall, 1846
Egan, Pierce, *Book of Sports and Mirror of Life*, W.Tegg and Co, 1836
Gale, Frederick, *Echoes from Old Cricket Fields*, Simpkin, Marshall, 1871
Gale, Frederick, *The Game of Cricket*, Swan Sonnenschein, Lowrie, 1887
Glover, William, *The Memoirs of a Cambridge Chorister*, Hurst and Blackett, 1885
Glover, William, *Reminiscences of Half a Century*, Hurst and Blackett, 1889
Green, Benny, *A History of Cricket*, Guild Publishing, 1988
Griffiths, Peter, and Kit Bartlett, *John Wisden: His Record Innings by Innings*, ACS Publications, 1999
Harris, Lord and F.S.Ashley-Cooper, *Kent Cricket Matches 1719–1880*, Gibbs and Sons, 1929
Heavens, Roger, *An Index to Frederick Lillywhite's Cricket Scores and Biographies, Volumes 1 to 5*, Roger Heavens, various years
Major, John, *More than a Game*, Harper Collins, 2007
Martin, R., *West Malling Inns, Beerhouses and their Keepers*, Snodland, 2006
Milton, Howard, *Cricket Grounds of Kent*, ACS Publications, 1992
Morrah, Patrick, *Alfred Mynn and the Cricketers of his Time*, Eyre and Spottiswoode, 1968
Pilch, Fuller, *The Whole Art of Cricket*, W.S.Fortey, 1870
Pilch, Fuller, *The Whole Art of Cricket*, G.Ingram, 1875
Pycroft, James, *The Game of Cricket*, Longmans, 1851
Reaney, P.H. and R.M.Wilson, *A Dictionary of English Surnames* (Third Edition), Oxford University Press, 1997
Underdown, David, *Start of Play*, Penguin Books, 2000
Warner, Sir Pelham, *Lord's: 1787–1945*, Harrap, 1947
Warner, Sir Pelham, *Gentlemen v Players: 1806–1949*, Harrap, 1950
Warner, H.W., *The Story of Canterbury Cricket Week*, J.A.Jennings Ltd, 1960
West, G.Derek, *The Elevens of England*, Darf, 1988
Wilde, Simon, *Number One: The World's Best Batsmen and Bowlers*, Vista, 1999
Wynne-Thomas, Peter, *George Parr: His Record Innings by Innings*, ACS Publications, 1993
Wynne-Thomas, Peter, *The History of Cricket: From the Weald to the World*, The Stationery Office, 1997

4 Journals and websites

Henderson, Peter, *Cricket in Canterbury since 1836: A History of Beverley Cricket Club*, www.polofarm.org/cricket

Howat, G.M.D. 'Fuller Pilch (1804 -1870)' in *Oxford Dictionary of National Biography*, Oxford University Press, 2004, reference number 22263

Taylor, Terry, 'Fuller Pilch: The Champion of Bury St Edmunds' in *Cricket Lore*, 5 (6), 2000, pp 38-41

Warsop, Keith, 'Bowling Evolution: From Rolling to Pitching' in *The Cricket Statistician*, 150, 2010, pp 21-24

Warsop, Keith, 'Batting evolution – its effect on run-scoring' in *The Cricket Quarterly*, 4, 1966, pp 203-210

Wisden Cricketers' Almanack

Wynne-Thomas, Peter, The Early County Championship, in *The Cricket Statistician*, 32, 1980, pp 2-7

cricketarchive.com
www.nationalarchives.gov.uk/currency
www.nationaltrustnames.org.uk

Note: Fuller Pilch was one of some sixty cricketers who were among the 54,900 subjects in the *Oxford Dictionary of National Biography*, published in 2004. Gerald Howat reported there in his article on Pilch that in 1870, shortly before his death, 'he published his *Whole Art of Cricket*, a brief manual of instructions on how to bat and bowl'.

In 1875, four years after Fuller's death, a coaching manual was published with the title *The Whole Art of Cricket*. It contained 'instructions on how to bat and bowl and directions to wicket-keeper, long-stop, short-slip, and each member of the cricket field by the late Fuller Pilch.' At the conclusion of the text the name J.Roche appears, which suggests that the contents had been written during Fuller's retirement. The date of composition can be confirmed as preceding 1864, the year that MCC legalised over-arm bowling, as Fuller's instructions to bowlers only refer to round-arm and under-arm bowling.

Five years earlier, another book with the same title had appeared, but without any names attached. The text of both books is almost identical, which raises the question why there was no attempt in 1870 to capitalise on Fuller's reputation. His declining health and 'Victorian values' regarding his involvement with William's bankruptcy may have played a part in the publisher's decision to keep the authorship anonymous.

Sadly, the text of these booklets give no indication that Fuller Pilch's own views had been taken into account in compiling the advice and there are no references which suggest 'my way' or 'in my experience' or anything as revealing as 'when facing a bowler like Lillywhite'.

THE WHOLE ART OF CRICKET,

WITH INSTRUCTIONS HOW TO BAT AND BOWL.

AND DIRECTIONS TO

WICKET KEEPER, LONG STOP, SHORT SLIP,

AND EACH MEMBER OF THE CRICKET FIELD BY THE LATE

FULLER PILCH.

TOGETHER WITH THE LAWS OF CRICKET AS LAID DOWN BY THE

MARYLEBONE CLUB.

London:—G. INGRAM, 124, Old Street, St. Luke's, E.C.

The front page of the instruction booklet apparently ghosted for Fuller Pilch and published five years after his death.

Appendix
Career Statistics

The statistical details given below relate to Fuller Pilch's performances in matches identified as first-class by the Association of Cricket Statisticians and Historians and listed in its 1996 publication *Complete First-Class Match List: Volume I, 1801-1914*.

First-class cricket: Batting and Fielding

	M	I	NO	R	HS	Ave	100	50	Ct
1820	1	2	0	2	2	1.00	-	-	1
1827	4	7	1	118	38*	19.66	-	-	3
1828	4	8	1	208	56	29.71	-	1	2
1829	4	8	0	43	18	5.37	-	-	6
1830	6	10	2	235	70*	29.37	-	1	1
1831	4	7	1	50	16	8.33	-	-	1
1832	7	12	3	287	50	31.88	-	1	8
1833	8	15	0	146	34	9.73	-	-	3
1834	7	12	3	551	153*	61.22	2	3	2
1835	3	4	0	106	59	26.50	-	1	1
1836	11	21	1	284	44	14.20	-	-	10
1837	10	15	1	372	84	26.57	-	2	8
1838	7	11	0	275	64	25.00	-	2	1
1839	8	13	2	258	41	23.45	-	-	4
1840	8	15	0	224	63	14.93	-	1	2
1841	10	17	1	413	67	25.81	-	2	6
1842	12	23	3	390	98	19.50	-	2	6
1843	10	18	3	371	57*	24.73	-	1	4
1844	16	32	3	517	50	17.82	-	1	7
1845	17	31	4	569	117	21.07	1	2	10
1846	10	17	1	182	31*	11.37	-	-	3
1847	12	22	1	385	49*	18.33	-	-	9
1848	6	11	0	178	54	16.18	-	1	4
1849	14	27	0	297	35	11.00	-	-	6
1850	8	15	1	255	51	18.21	-	2	4
1851	9	17	0	274	54	16.11	-	2	4
1852	6	12	0	71	26	5.91	-	-	1
1853	5	10	0	42	12	4.20	-	-	2
1854	2	4	0	44	32	11.00	-	-	-
Totals	**229**	**416**	**32**	**7147**	**153***	**18.61**	**3**	**24**	**122**

Notes: In his career as a whole, Pilch was dismissed 179 times bowled(47%); 154 times caught (40%); 25 times run out (7%); 17 times stumped (4%); eight times lbw (3%) and once hit wicket. He was dismissed most often by William Lillywhite, 49 times in all.

First-class cricket: Fifties (27)

Score	For	Opponent	Venue	Season
56	England[2]	Yorks, Notts and Leics	Sheffield	1828
70*	Suffolk[1]	MCC	Lord's	1830
50	Cambridge Town[1]	MCC	Lord's	1832
87*	Norfolk[1]	Yorkshire	Norwich	1834
73	Norfolk[2]	Yorkshire	Norwich	1834
105*	England[1]	Sussex	Brighton	1834
153*	Norfolk[2]	Yorkshire	Sheffield	1834
60	Players[1]	Gentlemen	Lord's	1834
59	England[1]	Kent	Lord's	1835
69*	Kent[2]	Sussex	Brighton	1837
84	Sussex[2]	England	Brighton	1837
64	South[1]	North	Lord's	1838
60	Kent[2]	Sussex	Brighton	1838
63	Kent[2]	Nottinghamshire	Town Malling	1840
53	Kent[1]	Sussex	Brighton	1841
67	Kent[1]	Sussex	Town Malling	1841
98	Kent[1]	England	Canterbury	1842
60	England[1]	Nottinghamshire	Trent Bridge	1842
57*	Kent[1]	England	Canterbury	1843
50	Gents of Notts[1]	Players of Notts	Trent Bridge	1844
54	Kent[2]	Sussex	Brighton	1845
55	Hampshire[1]	MCC	Brighton	1845
117	West[1]	MCC	Bath	1845
54	Kent[1]	England	Canterbury	1848
51	Kent[2]	England	Canterbury	1850
50	All England XI[2]	MCC	Lord's	1851
54	Kent[1]	Sussex	Hove	1851

First-class cricket: Bowling

Pilch's bowling performances were recorded far less comprehensively than his batting. For most of his career, even in very important matches, scorers only rarely recorded details of bowlers' performances, such as overs bowled and runs conceded. Bowlers were often not credited with wickets taken when batsmen were dismissed caught or stumped. Where details were recorded they were often not published. From time to time researchers find details of old matches, so there is still a prospect of filling in some of the many gaps.

In first-class matches Pilch is currently recorded as taking a total of 142 wickets, with 96 of them coming in the five seasons 1830 to 1834, the only years when he took more than ten wickets in a season. Some 88 per cent of all his wickets, 125 in all, were recorded as bowled. If only half of his wickets were bowled, not an unreasonable assumption, then he took perhaps 250 wickets or so in first-class games.

First-Class cricket: Five wickets or more in an innings (3)

Bowling	For	Opponent	Venue	Season
5-?	Suffolk	MCC[1]	Lord's	1830
5-?	Surrey	England[1]	Lord's	1831
7-?	L to Z	A to K[1]	Lord's	1833

Note: For the reasons given in the paragraphs above the table, Pilch may have taken five wickets in an innings on other occasions.

All Cricket: Batting

The figures given below relate to Fuller Pilch's performances in all matches, whether or not they are now treated as first-class. It is not possible to claim that they are comprehensive of course, and researchers will no doubt continue to find out details of new matches where Fuller took part, particularly minor games in the early part of his career. Because scorers only rarely recorded details of bowlers' performances, it is not possible to provide an equivalent table dealing with his bowling.

	M	I	NO	R	HS	Ave
1820	1	2	0	2	2	1.00
1821	1	2	1	8	8	8.00
1822	1	2	0	5	5	2.50
1823	1	2	0	12	12	6.00
1824	4	7	1	122	51	20.33
1825	3	4	0	107	69	26.75
1826	7	12	3	382	82*	42.44
1827	8	14	0	255	48	18.21
1828	8	15	0	409	56	27.26
1829	12	24	2	335	42	15.22
1830	13	24	3	506	127*	24.09
1831	13	24	2	501	65	22.77
1832	11	19	4	419	74	27.93
1833	11	19	1	391	115	21.72
1834	12	21	3	811	153*	45.05
1835	8	12	2	381	59	38.10
1836	18	33	4	780	107	26.89
1837	12	18	1	544	160	32.00
1838	13	23	1	486	67	22.09
1839	15	27	3	624	114	26.00
1840	17	31	1	521	63	17.36
1841	15	27	2	618	67	24.72
1842	19	34	4	593	98	19.77
1843	15	24	4	549	57*	27.45
1844	19	38	3	577	50	16.48
1845	22	40	4	649	117	18.02
1846	19	33	2	406	62	13.41
1847	24	42	3	678	49*	17.38
1848	11	19	1	250	54	13.88
1849	25	48	2	570	52	12.39
1850	19	34	4	453	52	13.22
1851	26	45	10	512	70	14.62
1852	9	16	1	118	26	7.86
1853	10	17	1	113	16	7.06
1854	4	7	0	54	32	7.71
1855	2	3	0	23	17	7.66
Totals	**428**	**852**	**73**	**13764**	**160**	**17.68**

Sources: cricketarchive.com, *Scores and Biographies*, and polofarm.org

Index

A page number in bold indicates an illustration.

Adams, T.M. 51, 55, 75, 104, 106, 118, 123, 125
Adelphi Hotel, Sheffield 113
Aislabie, Benjamin 26, 51, 57, 74
Albert of Saxe-Coburg and Gotha, Prince 92
Allen, Sir G.O.B. 115
Angel Inn, Bury St Edmunds, Suffolk 20, 27
Ashby, T. 22, 24
Ashley-Cooper, F.S. 65
Atherstone, Warwickshire 105
Atherton, M.A. 7
averages first published 10
Aylesford Club, Kent 93

Baker, I.G.A. 79
Baker, Rev John 67, 74
Baker, W. de C. 67, 72, 74, 83, 118, 119
Baldock, William 79
Banbury, Oxfordshire 109
bankruptcy in wine and beer trade 127
Banks, Edward 92-94, 122
Banks, W.J. 92, 93, 96
Barker, Thomas 53, 80, 98
'Barn-Door' match 57
Barnsley, Yorkshire 119
Barnes's Rooms, Canterbury 74, 77
Bat and Ball Inn, Canterbury 96
Bath, Somerset 89
batting averages, 1780-1826 11
batting averages, 1828-1843 13
batting averages, 1837-1841 55
Bayley, Rev Sir J.R.L.E. 77, 122
Bayley, Sir John 69, 79, **98**, 110
Beagley, Thomas 22, 24, 30, 32
Bear Inn, Lewes, Sussex 69
Beauclerk, Rev Lord Frederick 57, 64, 74
Beehive Ground, Walworth 86, 91
Beeston, John 18
'Bell's Life' newspaper 10, 60, 61, 77, 99, 102, 113, 125
Bessborough, (sixth) Earl of *see* Ponsonby
Beverley Club, Canterbury 6, 67, 70, 78, 81-83, 93, 96, 127

Beverley Ground, Canterbury 76-78, 81, 85, 86, **88**
Bickley, John 110, 115
Birmingham 98, 102, 105, 107, 110
Blake, W. 26
Bligh, Hon and Rev E.V. 119
Blunt, F.S. 54
Botham, Sir I.T. 5
Bowdler, Charles 76
Box, Thomas 70, 79, 83, 84, 89, **98**, 100, 105, 118
Boycott, Geoffrey 3
Bradford, Yorkshire 102, 107, 110
Brand, John 19, 26
Brighton, Sussex 13, 24, 27, 30, 40, 45, 49, 52, 53, 57, 58, 62-64, 66, 69, 74-76, 80, 82-84, 87-90, 92, 94, 96, **98**, 100
Broadbridge, James 12, 22, 24, 25, 27-31
Bromley, Kent 45, 48, 69, 72, 80, 92
Brown, George 87, 89, 90, 94, **98**, 111
Brunswick Ground, Hove 102, 104, 107, 109, 111, 118
Bury St Edmunds, Suffolk 18-21, 24-29, 31-33, 98, 105, 128
Buttress, William 113

Caffyn, William 5, 113
Caldecourt, W.H. 16, 17, 22, 24, 31, 34, 38, 39, 46, **98**, 107
Camberwell, Hall's ground 47, 60
Cambridge 6, 18, 20, 34, 46, 95, 103-104
Cambridge University 26, 74
Canterbury, Kent 68, 70, 74, 81-85, 87, 89, 94, 96-98, 102, 107, 108, 110-112, 114, 117, 118, 120, 121, 128, 129, **129**, 132
Canterbury Cavalry Barracks 68, 96
Canterbury Christ Church University 132
Canterbury Club 67
Canterbury Cricket Week 6, 74, 76, 81-85, 89, 93, 97, 98, 105, 107, 110, 112, 114, 115, 118, 119, 127

142

Index

'catapulta' bowling machine 16
Census 1841 69
Census 1851 82
Census 1861 118, 119
Chalvington, Sussex 63, 66
Championship of England 5, 28, 60, 61, 92
Chatham, Kent 118, 119
Chatteris, Cambridgeshire 34
Cheslyn, Lt Richard 25, 51
Chichester, Sussex 111
Chilston Park, Kent 67
Chislehurst, Kent 34, 35, 39, 45, 52, 58
Christ Church Cricket Ground, Oxford 109, 111, 113
Christopher, Amelia 107
Clarke, William 56, 68, 79, 89, 91, 94, 97, 102, 104, 106, 110-114, 115
Cleaver, Capt 83
Clifford, William 67-70
Cobbett, James 34, 47, 62, 70
Copenhagen House Inn, Islington 92
Coronation of Queen Victoria 62
Country-house cricket 67
Court of Bankruptcy, London 128
Coventry, Warwickshire 102
Crabbett Park, Worth, Sussex 49, 54
Cranbrook, Kent 107, 109, 118
'Cricketer's Alphabet' 85
Crimean War 7
Cronje, W.J. ('Hansie') 6

Daft, Richard 15, 26, 120
Dark, J.H. 38, 39, 57, 76, 91, 97
Darlington, Co Durham 107
Darnall New Ground, Sheffield 21
Dartford Brent, Kent 34
Dawson, G.E. 22
Dean, James sen 77, 79, 91, 92, **98**, 104, **100**
Dearman, James 40, 43, 53, 60, 61
Deedes, William 78
Denison, William 5, 81
Derby 102, 105, 127
Dereham, Norfolk 3 2, 33, 35
Dickens, C.J.H. (author) 49, 50, 91, 127
Dilshan Dilscoop 14
'Dombey and Son' 91
Dorrinton, William 69, 72, 79, 91, **100**, 102, 106, 123
Douglas, J.S. 67
Dragoons (Thirteenth) 68
draw (batting stroke) 14
Ducie, (first) Earl of 35
Duckworth Lewis Method 59

Dudlow, J.N. 72
Duncton, Sussex 80

East Kent Cricket Club 108
Edinburgh, Midlothian 110
Egan, Pierce 18, 37
Englebright, George 45
Eton College 81, 122
Eton, Brocas meadows 84
experimental round-arm matches 21, 22, **23**

Fagge, Rev J.F. 123, 124
Felix, Nicholas 13, 16, 51, 56, 67, 68, 75-77, 87, 89, 92, 94, 96, 99, **100**, 101-107, 111, 123, 124, 126, 133
Fellowes, H.W. 104, 107
Fenner, F.P. 46, 78
Fennex, William 20
Fitzgerald, R.A. 119
Fitzwilliam, Hon C.W.W. 99
'flamingo' batting stroke 14
'Flashman, Sir H.P.' 75
Fleece Hotel, Canterbury 130
Folkestone, Kent 118
Forest Ground, Nottingham 53
Fountain Hotel, Canterbury 78
Fuller, Bayfield 9
Fuller, Ben 9
Fuller, Frances 9
Fuller, James 9
Fuller, John 9

Gale, Frederick 6, 7, 14, 15, 49-51, 55, 64, 65, 77, 84, 86, 89, 93, 106, 120, 121, 128, 129
George IV, King 7
George Field, West Malling 34, 46
George Inn, West Malling 31, 46, **47**
Glasgow, Lanarkshire 110
Globe Tavern, Canterbury 82
Glover, Julia (actor) 74
Glover, William 34
Godalming, Surrey 31
Good, Bartholomew 47
Grace, H.M. 119
Grace. E.M. 119, 120
Grace, Martha (née Pocock) 119
Grace, W.G. 17, 119, 120
Grafton, (fourth) Duke of 20
Gravesend, Kent 16, 52, 69, 87, 91, 92, 102, 104, 114
Gravesend, Victoria Gardens 16
Grundy, James 112, 113, 115
Guy, Joseph 56, 80, **100**, 105, 124

143

Index

Hambledon, Hampshire 17, 20
Hankey, Col H.A. 83
Hardesty, George 61
Harris, David 11
Harris, (third) Baron 46, 65
Harris, (fourth) Baron 65
Hawkes, ?. 53
Hawkins, Charles 68, 79
Hemsted Park, Benenden 31, 46, 50, 62, 83
Hereford 113
Hervey-Bathurst, Sir F.H.H. 57
Hill of Almaraz, (first) Viscount 68
Hillyer, W.R. 51, 65, 68, 70, 113, 123, 126
Hodges, T.L. 31, 46, 83
Holroyd, Edward 128
Holt, Norfolk 9, 18, 27
Horningtoft, Norfolk **8**, 9, **10**, 130
Horningtoft Heritage Society **100**, 131
Houghton, W. 111
Hove, Sussex 102, 104, 106-107, 111, 114, 115
Howard, T.C. 22
Howard, ?. 45
Howat, G.M.D. 137
Huddersfield, Yorkshire 110
Hull, Yorkshire 104
Hyde Park, Sheffield 39, 40, 45, 94

Ibbetson, J.R. 94
Ilkeston, Derbyshire 110

Jupp, Henry 120

Kennington Oval 92, 96, 97, 102, 105, 106, 107, 109-111, 114, 118
Kent County Cricket Club formation 118
Kent Cricket Club formation 78, 83, 85, 91
King's Dragoon Guards (First) 83
King's Lynn, Norfolk 9, 110, 111, 119
King William Tavern, Sheffield 119
Knight, G.T. 22, 24-26

Laws, O. 45
Laws of Cricket 7, 12, 13, 25, 47, 105
Leamington Spa, Warwickshire 105
Leech, Charles 27, 28
Leeds, Kent 34, 35, 51, 62, 67, 81, 82
Leeds, Yorkshire 94, 98, 99, 105
Leicester 27, 28, 36, 49, 52, 53, 79, 83, 84, 98, 105

Lillywhite, F.W. 12, 14, 15, 22, 25, 27-30, 32-35, 36, 43, 45, 52, 53, 56-58, 62-65, 68-70, 76-80, 89, 91, 92, 97, 98, **100**, 103, 105, 125
'Little Dorrit' 127
Liverpool, Lancashire 87, 98, 127
Lord's Cricket Ground 5, 6, 9, 12, 13, 16, 20, 22, 24, 25, 27, 29-32, 34-37, 43, 45, 47-51, 55, 57, 60, 62-64, 68-70, 74-76, 82-84, 87, 88, 91, 93, 96, 97, **98**, 102, 104, 107, 109-111, 114, 118, 119
Louth, Lincolnshire 107

Macawin, E. 99
Magdalen Ground, Oxford 113
Maidenhead Inn, Oxford 106, 108
Maidstone, Kent 118
Maidstone Gaol 127, 128
Malton, Yorkshire 107
Manchester, Lancashire 87, 94, 98, 100, 102, 105, 107, 110, 127
Marsden, Thomas 22, 24, 27, 28, 30, 36-40, 43, 45, 47, 60, 91
Martin, Edward 103, 106, 108, 111, 115
Martingell, William 69, 81, 82, 83, 85, 87, 89, 92-94, 96, 100, 102, 106, 111, 118, 123
Martyn, Wykeham 65
MCC 7, 12, 13, 16, 19, 21, 22, 24, 27, 29-33, 36, 37, 49-52, 57, 63, 64, 69, 70, 74, 79, 82-85, 87, 91, 92, 107, 109, 111, 119
MCC Jubilee Match, 1837 57
Matthews (or Mathews), William 19-22, 24, 31
Midhurst, Sussex 31, 80
Mileham, Norfolk 108
Mills, Richard 45, 69
Milner, Col Charles 93, 97
Milton, Viscount 99
Mitcham, Surrey 81
Mordaunt, Louisa (actor) 74, 76
Morrah, Patrick 61
Mortlock, T.S. 114
Munn, W.A. 79
Mynn, Alfred 5, 34-36, 40, 43, 45-47, 51, 52, 55, 56, 60-62, 65-67, 69, 70, 72, 75, 76, 78-80, 82-84, 89, 92, 97, 99, 100, 103, 104, 106, 107, 111, 115, 118, 119, 122-125, 126
Mynn, W.P. 68-70, 75, 77, 82, 122, 124

Nackington Estate, Canterbury 96
Napoleon Bonaparte 7

144

Index

Newburgh, Aberdeenshire 110
Newcastle-upon-Tyne, Northumberland 99
New Kent Club 93
Newland, Capt 83
Newmarket, Suffolk 113
Nisbett, Louisa (actor) 74, 76
Norton, Silas 46
Norton, W.S. 119, 120
Northampton 112
Norwich, Norfolk 9, 27, 29, 32, 36, 40, 43, 46, 49, 52, 127, 128
Nottingham 49, 52-54, 72, 79, 84, 89, 94, 98

Old Stagers 78, 127
Onslow, D. 19
Orange Theatre, Canterbury 74, 77-78
Overend, Gurney and Co Ltd (bank) 127
Oxford 103, 104, 106, 108, 111, 113-114

Packer 'World Series' cricket 6
Parker's Piece, Cambridge 35, 46, 95
Parnther, C.H. 46
Parr, George 87, 92, 100, 101, 105, 107, 109, 110, 112, 115
Pell, O.C. 99, **100**
Penshurst, Kent 64, 68, 69, 81 ,115,
Peterborough, Northamptonshire 107
Petworth Park, Sussex 84
'Pickwick Papers' 49, 50
Pilch, Alfred (great nephew) 85, 107, 117, 128
Pilch, Frances (née Fuller) (mother) 9
Pilch, Frances (sister) 9

Pilch, Fuller
  addresses in Canterbury 107, 128
  averages for Kent, 1837-1841 55, 56
  bankruptcy of nephew William 127, 128
  baptism record **10**
  bat maker 91, 106, 107, **108, 115,** 117
  batting against William Lillywhite 14, 15, 22, 27
  batting lessons 15
  batting stance 16, **41, 59**
  benefit 64
  bicentenary festival, 2004 131, **132**
  birth 9
  'catapulta' 16, 17
  Champion of England 5, 28, 36-39
  coaching at Cambridge 34, 46
  coaching at Canterbury 82, 86
  coaching at Kings's School, Canterbury 118
  coaching at Oxford 103, 106, 108
  contract with Beverley Club 78, 79
  Clarke and Wisden dispute 112, 113
  death 128
  drinking during matches 51
  early development at Sheffield 18
  education 108
  fiftieth birthday 114
  first century 31
  first century at Lord's 43
  first-class averages, 1830-1839 66
  forward play 13, 15
  funeral 129
  gambling 6
  game with officers and men at Canterbury Cavalry Barracks 83
  ground at West Malling 52
  grave blocks Concert Hall plans 132
  hat knocked on wicket 57
  highest innings 57
  illnesses 84, 102, 111, 127
  instruction manuals 137, **138**
  joins Bury Cricket Club 18
  joins Norwich Cricket Club 32
  joins Town Malling Cricket Club 46
  joins Clarke's All-England Eleven 98
  Kent debut 52
  landlord of George Tavern, West Malling 46
  love of Kent 65
  matches:
    Alfriston v The Priory 68
    (Clarke's) All-England XI v XIV, XV, XVI, XVIII, XX or XXII Players 94, 98-100, 102, 104, 106-111; v Surrey 110; v Surrey and Sussex 110
    Benenden v Kent 46, 50 51; v Hollingbourne 114
    Beverley v Dover 70; v Leeds 82; v Leeds Park 82; v Penshurst 115; v Swingate 82; v Woodnesborough 96
    Brinton v Litcham 32, 33
    Buckinghamshire v Berkshire 84
    Bury St Edmunds v Biggleswade 18, 19; v Cambridge University 20, 21; v Eleven Gentlemen from Newmarket, Cambridge and Saffron Walden 20; v MCC 26, 27, 29, 31-33; v Melford 20; v Newmarket 19; v Nottingham 19, 20; v Pattiswick 19; v Saffron Walden 20; v Woodbridge 30, 31
    Bury and Suffolk v MCC 97, 98

145

Index

Cambridgeshire *v* MCC 34
Cambridge Town *v* MCC 35
Canterbury Club *v* Manchester 110
Chalvington *v* Brighton 63, 64, 66, 74-76
Chilston *v* Beverley 67, 68
Dover *v* Beverley 70
East Kent/Kent Club *v* Stilebridge 107; *v* West Kent 82
Eleven Players engaged at Oxford as bowlers *v* Oxford University 113
Eleven Players *v* XVIII Gentlemen of Surrey Club 114; *v* XVII Gentlemen 24
England *v* Kent 43, 45, 48, 52; *v* Kent and Sussex 51; *v* Nottinghamshire 98; *v* Nottinghamshire and Sussex 64; *v* Sussex 21, 22, **23** 27, 30, 34, 36, 40, 42, 43, 45, 83, 94, 100; *v* The 'B's' 27, 32; *v* Three Counties 18, 28
England XI *v* Five Gentlemen of Southwell and Six Nottinghamshire Professionals 94
Fast Bowlers *v* Slow Bowlers 69, 70, **71**
Gentlemen *v* Players 30, 62
Gentlemen of England *v* Cambridge Town 95; *v* Gentlemen of Hampshire 30; *v* Gentlemen of Kent 35; *v* Old Etonians 70
Gentlemen of Kent *v* MCC 58
Gentlemen of Nottinghamshire *v* Players of Nottinghamshire 84
Gentlemen of Sussex *v* MCC 64; *v* Players of Sussex 63
Goodwood *v* West Sussex 68
Gravesend *v* Bearstead 87; *v* Islington Albion Copenhagen Club 91, 92
Hampshire *v* England 80; *v* MCC 83, 84, 87, 89
Hastings and St Leonards *v* Tunbridge Wells 68
Hollingbourne *v* West Wickham 115
Holt *v* Nottingham 18
Kent *v* Benenden 62; *v* XVIII of Tunbridge Wells 115; *v* England 64, 65, 68-70, 72, **73**, 74, 75, 77, 80, 83, 84, 87, 89, 93, 96, 97, 102, 104, 105, 107, 109, 111-114; *v* MCC 114; *v* Nottinghamshire 57, 68, 72, 87; *v* XVI of Oxfordshire 104; *v* Surrey 92, 93, 96, 97, 105, 107, 111, 114; *v* Sussex 52, 53, 56, 57, 62-64, 69, 70, 74, 75, 82, 83, 87, 89, 92, 93, 96, 97, 102, 104, 107, 109, 110, 112; *v* (Clarke's) All-England Eleven 104, 107, 109; *v* Yorkshire 104
Kent and Sussex *v* (Clarke's) All-England Eleven 114
Kent Club *v* Sevenoaks Vine 109; *v* South London Club 86, 91, 94, 96, 98
Leeds *v* Dartford 34
Leeds and Bearstead *v* Dartford 35
Leicester *v* Sheffield 27
Liverpool *v* Manchester 87
L-Z *v* A-K 36
MCC *v* England 32, 64, 82; *v* Sussex 50, 52, 57, 58, 62, 63, 84, 87, 89; *v* Gentlemen of Kent 34, 36, 39; *v* Midland Counties 82, 83; *v* Petworth 84; *v* The 'B's 27; *v* North 74, 79, 83, 84, 87, 89
Norfolk *v* MCC 9, 18, 29, 30, 32, 33, 83, 84, 89, 90, 93, 95, 98; *v* Yorkshire 40, 43, **44**, 45, 52, 53
North *v* South 51, 52
Norwich *v* Brinton 36, 40; *v* MCC 32; *v* Rest of Norfolk 36
Nottingham *v* XXII of New Forest & Bingham Club 53, 54
Old *v* Young 107, 110
Penshurst *v* Benenden 64, 69
Pilch's All-England XI *v* Nottinghamshire 79, 89; *v* XVI of Oxfordshire 111, 113; *v* Felix's XI 92
Players *v* Gentlemen 29, 31, 32, 35, 45, 47, 52, 57, 64, 68, 70, 76, 82, 84, 87, 88, 90, 94, 97, 102, 104; *v* XVI Gentlemen 57
Right Handed *v* Left Handed 27, 47
Shillinglee *v* Brighton 80, 82
Single *v* Married 29, 84, 104
Slow Bowlers *v* Fast Bowlers 68, 75
South *v* North 57, 62, 104, 105, 109
(Clarke's) South XI *v* (Clarke's) North XI 114
Suffolk *v* MCC 24, 27, 29, 30; *v* Norfolk 9, 29
Surrey *v* England 32, *v* MCC 83; *v* Sussex 30, 31
Sussex *v* England 58, 62, 68, 69, 80
Town Malling *v* Benenden 31, 63; *v* Chislehurst and Bromley 45; *v* Gravesend 69; *v* Kent 48, 51, 52; *v*

Leeds 62; *v* Leeds and Bearstead 34;
v Penshurst 68; *v* Reigate 57, 58
Tunbridge Wells *v* Sevenoaks 72
Twenty-Two of Lynn *v* Lynn 110
Updown *v* MCC 69
West of England *v* MCC 83, 84, 89
Western Counties *v* MCC 87
Worth *v* Uckfield 54
memorial and fund 130, 131
Norfolk career record 99
pension 127
parlour at the Saracen's Head 121
photograph **118**
'Poke' shot 14, 124
replacement headstone **131,** 132
Suffolk spirit 18
Sussex offer 65
umpire 66, 72, 81, 114, 118, 119
use of unspliced bat **41**, 45, **59**, 106, 108

Pilch, Hephzibah (nephew's wife) 85, 107, 117, 128
Pilch, John Fuller (brother) 9
Pilch, Nathaniel (father) 9
Pilch, Nathaniel (eldest brother) 9, 10, 32, 36, 38, 43, 52, 53, 99
Pilch, Peter 132
Pilch, William (elder brother) 9, 10, 18, 31, 32, 36, 38, 43, 45, 52, 98, 99, 110, 119
Pilch, William (nephew) 10, 40, 69, 85-87, 89, 91-93, 96, 97, 102, 104, 107-109, 117, 122, 127, 128
Pilch, Susanna (sister) 9
Pilch's Ground, Town Malling 52, 55
Ponsonby, Hon F.G.B. 74, 76, 79, 92
Portsmouth, Hampshire 113
Preston Hall, Aylesford 93, 97
Prince of Wales Ground, Oxford 103, 104, 106, 108
Prowse W.J. 56, 125
Pycroft, Rev James 91

railways 7, 91
Rawlins, George 28
Redgate, Samuel 17, 46, 47, 52, 53, 57, 58, 61-64, 68-70, 72, 74, 75, 84, 87, 89, 90, 92, 93
Repton, Humphry 99
Rideal, William 128
Rippingall, Squire 45
Rookes family 96
Ross-on-Wye, Herefordshire 109
Roughham Park, Suffolk 19

round-arm bowling 7, 11, 14
round-arm bowling trial matches 21, 22, **23**
Royal Oak Inn, King's Lynn 110, 119

St Gregory's Cemetery, Canterbury 129, 130, **131**, 132
St Lawrence Ground, Canterbury 78, 96, 97, 117, 118, 120, 127, 131
St Lawrence House, Canterbury 96
St Stephen's Field, Hackington, Canterbury 67
Saracen's Head Inn, Canterbury 7, 117, **120**, 121, 127, 128
Saunders, James 22, 24, 29, 30, 32, 46
Scott, Capt 83
Searle, William 22, 24, 29, 30
Selby, Thomas 16, 31, 34, 46, 48, 50, 52, 55, 50, 63-65
Sevenoaks, Kent 72, 109
Sewell, Thomas sen 79, 93, **100**
Sheffield, Yorkshire 13, 18, 20, 21, 27, 28, 38-40, 42, 45, 49, 53, 61, 94, 98, 104, 105, 107, 110 113, 119
Shillinglee Park, Sussex 80
Sims, J.M. 115
single-wicket Laws 37
Slater, William 24
Sleaford, Lincolnshire 111
Smith, G.T. 18
Sneller, John 68
Sondes, (fourth) Baron 65, 96
Southampton, Hampshire 80, 84, 89
South Eastern Railway 83, 93
Sparks, John 24
'stale men' 103
Stearman, William 65, 67
Stockton-on-Tees, Co Durham 99, 105
Stoke-on-Trent, Staffordshire 110
Stourbridge, Worcestershire 100
straight-arm bowling 12
Streatfeild, R.J. 120
Sussex C.C.C. formed 65
Swaffham Racecourse ground, Norfolk 9
Swann, E.G. 122

Taylor, C.G. 68, 76, 77, 78, **98**, 124
Taylor, Terry 131
Taylor, Tom (dramatist) 78
Thanet, (eleventh) Earl of 57
Thwaites, Edward 14
Townley, T.M. 99

Index

Town Malling, Kent 16, 36, 45, **47**, 49, **50**, 52, 55-57, 61-64, 66-70, 72, 76, 78, 79, 81, 129, 128, 130
Trent Bridge ground, Nottingham 72, 79, 87, 89
Tunbridge Wells, Kent 72, 89, 93, 97, 102, 105, 110, 112, 115, 118
Tunbridge Wells Racecourse ground 84
Twenty20 cricket 6-7, 13, 14, 28
Twisden Hodges, T. 46, 50, 65

Uckfield, Sussex 54
under-arm bowling 7, 11 14
United All-England Eleven 113
Updown, Kent 69

Victoria, Queen 7
Vincent, Emmanuel 40
Vivian, Sir R.H. (later first Baron Vivian) 25

Wanostrocht, Nicholas *see Felix*
Ward, William 18, 19
Warsop, Keith 11, 12, 13

Watts, G.F. 131
Wenman, E.G. 32, 45, 51, 55-58, 62, 64, 67, 69, 70, 72, 79, 80, 83, **98**, 106, 107, 109, 118, 119, 122-124, 126
Wentworth House, Rotherham, Yorkshire 99
West Malling, Kent *see Town Malling*
Weymouth, Dorset 105
White Hart Ground, Bromley, Kent 72
Whittaker, C.G. 75
Wilkinson, M.A. 107
Willsher, Edgar 111-113, 119, 123, 124
Winter's Farm, Canterbury 96
Winterton, (fourth) Earl 80, 82, 84
Wisbech, Cambridgeshire 108
Wisden, John 93, 104, 105, 107, 110, 112-115
Wisden Cricketers'Almanack 86, 130
Woolhouse, W.H. 21, 38, 39
Worcester 102, 110
Worth, Sussex 49
Wyatt, R.E.S. 115

York 98